CREDIT SCORE MASTERY

UNLOCK THE SECRETS TO RAPIDLY RAISING YOUR SCORE TO 800 AND BEYOND

KIRK TEACHOUT

Copyright © 2023 by Kirk Teachout. All rights reserved.

No part of this book may be reproduced in any form or by any electronic or mechanical means, including information storage and retrieval systems, without written permission from the author, except for the use of brief quotations in a book review.

First published by IV Quarter Publishing 2023

All rights reserved. No part of this publication may be reproduced, stored or transmitted in any form or by any means, electronic, mechanical, photocopying, recording, scanning, or otherwise without written permission from the publisher. It is illegal to copy this book, post it to a website, or distribute it by any other means without permission.

Kirk Teachout asserts the moral right to be identified as the author of this work.

Kirk Teachout has no responsibility for the persistence or accuracy of URLs for external or third-party Internet Websites referred to in this publication and does not guarantee that any content on such Websites is, or will remain, accurate or appropriate.

Designations used by companies to distinguish their products are often claimed as trademarks. All brand names and product names used in this book and on its cover are trade names, service marks, trademarks and registered trademarks of their respective owners. The publishers and the book are not associated with any product or vendor mentioned in this book. None of the companies referenced within the book have endorsed the book.

It is not intended to be a source of financial or legal advice. Making adjustments to a financial strategy or plan should only be undertaken after consulting with a professional. The publisher and the author make no guarantee of financial results obtained by using this book

CONTENTS

Introduction   5

1. Decoding the Credit Score Mystery   13
2. The Credit Score Superheroes   31
3. Conquering Credit Card Chaos   45
4. Debt Demolition: The Ultimate Battle Plan   69
5. Credit Repair: The Art of Bouncing Back   87
6. Skyrocket Your Score With Credit Building Hacks   109
7. Maintaining Your Soaring Credit Score   127
8. The Truth About Credit Scores: Myths, Misconceptions, and Mistakes   141
9. Bonus — Habits of the 800 Club: Secrets of the Credit Elite   149

Conclusion   165
Resources   171

INTRODUCTION

Building a good credit score is a total mystery to most young people and for good reason. They were never taught how to build a good credit score! Credit score mastery is not necessarily something most people think about, especially when they're in their 20s and 30s. The thing is, this is the perfect time to start thinking about how you're going to build up your credit score if you haven't started thinking about it already. You're still young, and you still have time to realize and alter any bad financial habits you might have. This means that building up a healthier credit score is well within your reach — even if you've accumulated a lot of debt over the years.

If you're struggling with debt build-up — from student loans, overdue credit card payments, or anything else —

just know you're not alone. Staying on top of your loans and various payments can be challenging, especially when you're also juggling expenses like rent, groceries, and eating out once in a while. Some people struggle to keep track of their spending habits, which can very quickly lead to them experiencing troubles with their finances and credit. Take the story of Issac and Miko, for example.

Issac and Miko were both in stable jobs. They both earned good salaries, and they believed they were managing their finances relatively well. They rarely indulged in expensive purchases, or splurged on things like impromptu shopping trips. However, despite their efforts, their spending habits left something to be desired. One night, after enjoying their weekly dinner outing at their favorite dim sum restaurant, Miko's credit card got declined.

Confused and embarrassed, they rushed home to check their account balance online and realized that they had somehow accumulated over $10,000 in credit card debt. Their financial situation had deteriorated without them even noticing it, which was obviously really scary and shocking for both of them. Issac and Miko had essentially become complacent in their spending habits, which meant they weren't paying enough attention to their day-to-day expenses.

Their story underscores just how crucial it is to learn financial responsibility and manage finances in a proactive way. If Isaac and Miko had been a little more mindful of their spending habits and kept better track of their credit card payments, they might not have found themselves in this situation. No matter how insignificant your purchases may seem, things like going out to dinner once a week and stopping by your favorite coffee shop every morning on your way to work can add up more quickly than you might think.

Despite the fact that the cost of living and inflation are on the rise (yes, these things are definitely anxiety-inducing), it's possible to avoid unnecessary financial stress — as long as you're willing to put the work in. Keeping track of your spending, staying vigilant about your debt payments, and checking your account balance regularly can help you avoid getting into situations like the one Isaac and Miko found themselves in.

If this book caught your eye, perhaps you're carrying an enormous amount of debt around with you and you'd like to figure out how you can raise your credit score despite that fact. If you've accumulated a huge amount of student loan debt (which is a common experience for those who decide to pursue a college education), you might feel like that debt is suffocating you, and like it's preventing you from living your life to the fullest. Your feelings of anxiety are valid, and again, you're not alone. I've been there, too, as have many of my friends and family members.

Things might feel insurmountable right now, but don't fret. Not all hope is lost. If you're worried about your financial future — if you recognize that maybe you haven't made the smartest financial decisions in the past, and you don't want to continue to make the same mistakes going forward — you've come to the right place. In fact, you've already made the right first step in wanting to take action. Simply thinking about how you're going to correct your financial habits and raise your credit score isn't enough. It's all about having the right information and tools on hand to be able to take action.

It took several years to accumulate the knowledge I'll be sharing with you in this book. I don't claim to have *all* the answers, but — having been in a situation similar to yours — I want to do everything I can to spread the information, stories, and tips that have ultimately changed my life for the better. One of the most helpful tips I learned during this process was that patience is a virtue. If you're currently buried in debt, it may take some time to get out of it and rebuild your credit. You've got to keep your eyes on the prize, though, because rebuilding your credit is absolutely possible, even when it feels like things have taken a turn for the worst.

For example, consider the story of Vicky Eves, the author of *I Beat Debt*. Vicky Eves grew up in a family where spending money they didn't have simply wasn't an option. She was brought up to be financially responsible and avoid taking on too much debt. However, after a few financial missteps, Vicky found herself drowning in debt. Because of this, her credit score took a major dive. Due to her poor credit score, Vicky was unable to open a regular bank account, which made her feel embarrassed and ashamed. She knew she had to take action right away if she was ever going to rebuild her credit.

She started by taking out a credit card for people who had poor credit and made sure to pay off the balance in full every single month. She also sought out information online, and used what she learned in her debt counseling sessions to get her financial situation back on track. Naturally, rebuilding her credit took some time, but Vicky was patient and eventually persevered. She refused to let her past mistakes define her financial future, and got over her fear of asking for financial advice when she needed it.

Today, Vicky is debt-free and has an excellent credit score. She wants others to know that it's possible to overcome financial setbacks — no matter how bad these setbacks may be — through determination, hard work, and, most importantly, patience. You, too, can be debt-free and obtain an excellent credit score. My aim, with this book, is to arm you with the tools and tips you'll need to do so.

Ten years ago, I found myself staring at a credit report that didn't seem, to me, like an accurate reflection of my financial life. Like many others, I didn't quite understand the complex world of credit scores, let alone how to improve them. My score at the time was far from impressive, and I knew that something had to change. That's when I embarked on a decade-long journey of meticulous research, trial and error, and diligent application of credit improvement techniques.

I spent countless hours analyzing credit reports, learning about the key factors that influence credit scores, and understanding the best practices of those with exceptional credit ratings. I reached out to wealthy individuals as well as devoured books and articles on the subject. Along the way, I discovered the powerful strategies and practical tips that I would later compile into this book.

As I applied these techniques to my own financial life, I watched in amazement as my credit score began to climb. Each month, I grew more excited as I inched closer to that elusive 800 mark. Finally, after years of determination and hard work, I achieved my goal: an exceptional credit score of 800. However, my journey didn't end there. I continued to refine my strategies and habits, keeping my credit score consistently above 800. My financial life was transformed, and the doors of opportunity opened wide before me.

Now, it's time for me to share this knowledge and these techniques with you. I hope to empower you with the tools you need to not only improve your credit score but also to join the ranks of the credit elite. Together, let's embark on this exciting journey toward exceptional credit and financial success.

1

DECODING THE CREDIT SCORE MYSTERY

The other day, my nephew, who's in his early twenties, was telling me all about how excited he was to move out of his parents' house and get his own apartment. He was working a steady job and had been saving up for a long time, so he felt pretty confident about his ability to secure a one-bedroom apartment that was within walking distance of his workplace. However, when he went to apply for the apartment, he was told that he needed to have a good credit score. My nephew was confused because he had never heard of a credit score before. He didn't know what it was or why it mattered.

Feeling frustrated and defeated, my nephew came to me for advice. I explained to him that a credit score is a number that represents his creditworthiness — basically, how likely he is to pay back a loan or credit card debt. I told him that landlords, lenders, and credit card companies use credit scores to determine whether or not to extend credit to someone. My nephew was surprised to hear this and realized that he had never been taught about credit scores in school or by his parents. He was determined to improve his credit score so that he could secure the apartment he wanted.

The next time he came over, I helped my nephew obtain a copy of his credit report and explained to him how to read it. We identified areas where he could improve, such as paying his bills on time and reducing his credit card balances to the best of his ability. We also discussed the importance of maintaining a good credit history and the ways in which his credit score could potentially impact his future financial goals.

With this newfound knowledge, my nephew took action and began to improve his credit score. He started making on-time payments, and was eventually able to pay down his credit card balances. He also set up automatic payments so that he wouldn't miss any future payment dates. In just a few months, his credit score had improved significantly, and he was able to get his dream apartment. Needless to say, I was incredibly proud and very happy for him.

One of the main reasons why so many people struggle with keeping their credit score up is that the concept of credit and maintaining a good credit score is severely misunderstood. I can't remember ever being taught about how to raise my credit score, and I realize now that it was probably somewhat of a mystery to my parents as well — which is why they weren't able to give me much advice or information on the topic. I believe this experience is pretty common among young people, especially those who don't happen to have a lot of life experience or financial responsibilities to keep track of.

To make matters worse, there's a lot of misinformation out there about what credit is and how it works. In fact, according to recent studies, around 65% of American adults think carrying a balance on their credit card is good for their credit. However, this belief couldn't be further from the truth. Carrying a balance actually hurts your credit score because it increases your credit utilization (i.e. the amount of credit you're using compared to the total amount you have available). A high credit utilization ratio essentially lets lenders know that you may be overextended and unable to manage your debt responsibly.

The aforementioned statistic shows just how much confusion there is surrounding credit among the general public. It's definitely understandable, especially considering how complex and overwhelming the world of credit can be, but you'll need to have a solid grasp of how credit actually works if you're going to make informed financial decisions. In this chapter, I'll delve into the various intricacies of credit and credit scores. This should hopefully demystify a few things so that you can start building up your credit right away without running into any confusion or unexpected issues.

WHAT IS A CREDIT SCORE?

As I mentioned previously, a credit score is essentially a numerical representation of one's creditworthiness, which is a measure of how likely they are to pay back their debts. Your credit score is calculated based on your credit history — which usually includes information like your credit utilization, your payment history, and the types of credit you have. Credit scores typically range from around 300 to 850, and the higher your credit score is, the more creditworthy you'll be according to landlords and credit card companies. This means that if your credit score is on the higher end, you'll be much more likely to get approved for things like apartments, credit cards, and loans.

There are a number of credit scoring systems that lenders and credit bureaus use, like FICO, for example. FICO is the most widely used credit scoring system, and its scores typically range from around 300 to 850. FICO scores are calculated using a complex algorithm, which takes a person's credit history and compares it to the credit history of millions of other people. There are some factors that can end up affecting your FICO score, like any recent credit inquiries you might have had, or the length of your credit history. A FICO score of 670 or higher is considered to be "good," however, you shouldn't necessarily settle for a "good" credit score. Having an excellent credit score is very important when it comes to maintaining your financial health, and it can open up a lot more opportunities for your future as well.

THE COMPONENTS OF A CREDIT SCORE

There are five key components that make up a credit score, namely payment history, amount owed, types of credit, credit history length, and new credit. Let's take a closer look at these components below, as these things can be a bit difficult to understand at first. If you're confused, don't worry! I'll be going into more detail in the next chapter.

Payment History

When it comes to determining a person's credit score, the most important factor is usually payment history. Your payment history represents your ability to pay your bills on time. Late or missed payments can significantly lower your credit score, while paying your bills on time every month can raise it.

Amount Owed

Another important factor that gets taken into consideration is the amount owed. The amount owed basically reflects your level of debt in comparison to your available credit. High levels of debt, especially in combination with maxed-out credit limits, can negatively impact your credit score.

Types of Credit

The types of credit you have can also affect your credit score. Having a mix of different types of credit — such as credit cards, mortgages, and loans — will demonstrate that you use your credit in a responsible way, which can help to boost your credit score.

Credit History

Your credit history is very important because it essentially shows lenders and landlords how long you've been using credit. In general, the longer your credit history is, the better your credit score will be. Basically, a long credit history demonstrates that you have a proven track record of using your credit responsibly.

New Credit

Opening several new credit accounts in a short amount of time can negatively impact your credit score, as it suggests that you oftentimes default on making payments on time. However, if you make credit inquiries that are related to rate shopping (i.e. let's say you're attempting to find the best mortgage or car loan rate), you shouldn't see any significant change in your credit score.

WHAT ISN'T INCLUDED IN CALCULATING CREDIT SCORES?

As you can see, there's a lot that gets taken into account when it comes to determining one's credit score. However, there are a few factors that are not included in the calculation of these scores. First of all, credit scores do not take a person's race, religion, or sex into account. This is because the Equal Credit Opportunity Act (ECOA) prohibits lenders and creditors from using these particular factors to determine creditworthiness. Instead, credit scores are based solely on a person's credit history and financial behavior.

Age is also not factored into the equation during the process of calculating credit scores. While it's true that credit history length is important, your credit history length is not the same thing as your age. Younger folks who have shorter credit histories can still have high credit scores, especially if they have a consistent record of paying their bills on time and using their credit responsibly.

One thing you might be concerned about is credit inquiries. However, you shouldn't worry too much about soft inquiries, as they won't impact your score. That said, hard inquiries, which tend to occur when a lender checks a person's credit history in response to a credit application, can have a temporary negative effect on your score. You should be able to get your score back up fairly quickly, though, so this isn't really something to stress about.

THE IMPACT YOUR CREDIT SCORE HAS ON YOUR FINANCIAL LIFE

Not a lot of people think about their credit score, because it's sort of "out-of-sight, out-of-mind." This makes sense, but it's not necessarily a good thing. Your credit score can impact your financial life in significant ways, which can in turn affect your personal life. One of the most common ways your credit score can affect your life is through the loan application process. If you have a low credit score, lenders might think you're not creditworthy and deny you the loan you're applying for. They may also charge you a higher interest rate, which is definitely not ideal.

Similarly, when applying for a mortgage, having a higher credit score can be extremely beneficial. The higher your credit score is, the lower your interest rate will be (in most cases), which means your mortgage payments will be more affordable. With a lower credit score, you're likely to be charged with a higher interest rate, which means your mortgage will probably end up costing way more than it should. Your credit score can also affect your retirement planning. Those with higher credit scores will be able to obtain more favorable interest rates on investments and loans, which will lead to higher returns on investments.

There are a few different types of credit scores: FICO, VantageScore, and industry-specific scores. FICO is the most commonly used credit score, and it ranges from about 300 to 850 (as previously discussed). VantageScore is a newer scoring system — which also ranges from 300 to 850 — with a higher score indicating better credit. Other industry-specific scores are specially designed to evaluate creditworthiness for particular purposes, such as car loans and insurance.

Why Are There Different Credit Scores?

There are different credit scores because various credit reporting agencies and financial institutions use different scoring models to evaluate a person's creditworthiness. These scoring models consider different factors and assign different weights to them, which means your credit score can vary depending on which credit agency you decide to go through.

For example, FICO considers a person's payment history, credit utilization, length of credit history, types of credit, and new credit inquiries in order to calculate their credit score. VantageScore, on the other hand, uses a different scoring model. While they consider pretty much the same factors, they assign different weights to them than FICO does. Moreover, industry-specific scores are designed to evaluate creditworthiness for specific purposes. As the name suggests, industry-specific scores consider factors that are specific to the industry. For example, if you want to take out a car loan, the lender might take your payment history, your use of credit, and your history of car loans into account when calculating your credit score.

Differences in credit scores can basically depend on the ways in which a certain credit reporting agency does things. There are three major credit reporting agencies in the United States, namely Equifax, Experian, and TransUnion. These agencies may have slightly different information about a person's credit history, which may lead to them calculating different credit scores for that person.

UNDERSTANDING THE CREDIT SCORE RANGE

Credit scores are typically broken down into a range of 300-850 and divided into five categories based on this range. These categories help lenders and other financial institutions determine the creditworthiness of a person like yourself fairly quickly. To give you a visual, the breakdown of the credit score range system usually looks something like this:

- Poor: 300-579
- Fair: 580-669
- Good: 670-739
- Very good: 740-799
- Exceptional: 800-850

The first category is the "poor" credit score range, which is between 300-579. People in this range are typically considered to be high-risk borrowers and may have difficulty obtaining credit. They're more likely to be charged high-interest rates and may be required to provide collateral or a co-signer in order to secure a loan.

The second category is the "fair" credit score range (580-669). This range is slightly better than the poor credit range but it still unfortunately indicates that the person attempting to borrow money may have a history of missed payments or high credit utilization. Borrowers in this range may still face higher interest rates and other restrictions when attempting to obtain credit.

The third category is the "good" credit score range (670-739). Borrowers in the "good" range are considered less risky and are more likely to be approved for credit at competitive interest rates. They may also qualify for special promotions and rewards programs. The "good" range is generally a solid place to be!

The fourth category is the "very good" credit score range, which is between 740-799. People in this range are considered to be excellent borrowers and are typically offered the best interest rates and terms possible. They also tend to have access to the most favorable rewards programs and promotions.

The final category is the "exceptional" credit score range (800-850). People in this range are generally considered to be the most creditworthy borrowers and they will typically be offered the lowest interest rates and most favorable terms. This is definitely the credit score range you want to aim for, though it might take some time to get there.

YOUR CREDIT REPORT: THE FOUNDATION OF YOUR CREDIT SCORE

While it may seem a little bit intimidating at first, breaking down the information in your credit report is a more straightforward process than you might think. Something I told my nephew when he was asking me about credit scores was that it's crucial that you review your credit report at least once a year in order to ensure its accuracy. This is also a great way to identify any errors or factors that may be negatively affecting your credit score.

Your credit report is divided into several different sections, which can be a bit overwhelming at first, but just take it one section at a time and you'll see that it's not so bad. The various sections of your credit report include personal information, credit accounts, payment history, public records, collection items, and any inquiries you may have had. One of the best things you can do for yourself when evaluating your credit report is to check for errors. Things like fraudulent accounts and incorrect payment histories can make your credit score drop, so it's important to dispute these errors if you want your credit score to be represented accurately.

What Do the Different Sections on Your Credit Report Mean?

Let's take a closer look at the sections you'll come across while reading your credit report. The fact that this information is separated into different sections makes the report a whole lot easier to read. It should also help you keep all of your information organized, so you won't lose or misplace details like your credit limit or the name of a certain lender.

Personal Information

This section of your credit report contains information like your name, your current and previous addresses, your date of birth, social security number, and other identifying factors. It also lists important details about your employment history, including your current and past employers. Your income will be listed in this section as well.

Credit History

This section provides information on your credit accounts (i.e. your credit cards, loans, and mortgages). For each of your accounts, it will show the name of the creditor or lender, the account number, the date the account was opened, the credit limit or loan amount, the balance owed, and your payment history. It will also show whether or not you have been delinquent or late on any payments, or if any of your accounts have been sent to collections.

Public Records

This section of your credit report includes any public records that are related to your credit history — such as bankruptcies, tax liens, and civil judgments. These records can have a significant effect on your credit score and can unfortunately stay on your credit report for several years after the fact.

Collection Items

This section shows your accounts (if any) that have been sent to collections due to a lack of payment. Any accounts that have been sent to collections can negatively impact your credit score, and like public records, this information can remain on your credit report for quite a long time.

Credit Inquiries

This section shows a list of companies or people who have accessed your credit report in the past two years. As I briefly mentioned, there are two types of inquiries: hard inquiries and soft inquiries. Hard inquiries tend to occur when you apply for credit, such as a loan or credit card, and this type of inquiry can end up lowering your credit score. Soft inquiries typically occur when you check your own credit report or when a certain company checks your credit report for promotional purposes. This type of inquiry will not have any impact on your credit score.

How to Get a Hold of Your Credit Report

You are entitled to receive a free credit report from each of the three major consumer reporting agencies (Equifax, Experian, and TransUnion) once a year. You can do this by visiting AnnualCreditReport.com. You have several options for requesting and reviewing your free credit report, as listed below:

- Visit AnnualCreditReport.com online
- Call (877) 322-8228 by phone
- Download and mail the Annual Credit Report Request form to the address provided on the site

You can choose to request all three reports at once or order one report at a time. If you'd like to monitor your credit report throughout the year, you can request the reports separately (one every four months). After receiving your annual free credit report, you can still request additional reports, but keep in mind that you may be charged a fee of no more than $14.50 by the credit reporting company, as required by law.

Credit Mastery Habit #1:

Action Step: Analyze your current credit report and identify your starting point.

To improve your credit score, you should start by reviewing your current credit report and identifying the most ideal starting point. You can establish a new credit mastery habit for yourself by obtaining a copy of your credit report from each of the three major credit bureaus, reading each report thoroughly, and gaining an understanding of the factors that have contributed or to are contributing to your credit score. Once you've evaluated your current score, you can determine where you need to start in terms of improving it. Signing up for monthly credit reporting from one of the bureaus could be a great way to help you track your progress over time as well as stay on top of any changes or updates to your credit report.

SEGUE

Now that you've got a deeper understanding of what credit is and how credit scores work, you should be able to read and evaluate your credit report and make more informed financial decisions. There are a lot of factors that get taken into account when your credit score gets calculated, and being in the know about these factors can help you stay on top of your credit score. In the next chapter, I'll dive deep into the key factors that can influence your credit score, as well as point you toward your next action step: creating a personalized action plan based on your unique credit profile.

2

THE CREDIT SCORE SUPERHEROES

I used to be embarrassed by my credit score. It seemed like everyone around me had fantastic credit, and I was the only one struggling to keep up for some reason. I realized that things had to change, and that I was the one who had to take control of my own financial situation. I started by taking a hard look at my finances (which, at the time, certainly had room for improvement). I then created a budget for myself and started keeping better track of my expenses. I realized that I was spending money on things I didn't need, which was making it difficult for me to pay my bills on time. So, I cut back on unnecessary expenses and started saving money.

Next, I made a plan to pay off my debts. I called my creditors and worked out manageable payment plans with each of them. I also started paying more than the minimum amount that was due each month so that I could reduce my balances faster. It was tough at first, but I stuck it out and eventually started to see some progress.

I was also able to build up my credit by opening another secured credit card. I made small purchases here and there, but I always paid them off in full each month to show that I was responsible with credit. As time went on, I was able to qualify for other lines of credit and my credit score started to improve.

It definitely wasn't an overnight process, but after a few months of hard work, I started to see real results. My credit score improved significantly, and I felt much more in control of my finances. This entire experience taught me that I have the power to take control of my financial future — and you do too! Allow me to share another story with you to further illustrate what I mean.

Erin Lowry, the author of the book *Broke Millennial*, was confident about her finances when she graduated from college. She had been using a credit card responsibly for four years and had no student loans to worry about. Her credit score was also pretty good. However, she faced difficulties when she and her roommate applied for an apartment in New York City. The apartment broker ran her credit report and found out that Lowry had a "thin file," which means that her credit card wasn't reporting activity to all three credit bureaus.

To fix her thin file, Lowry decided to get a second credit card, and was fortunately approved for the apartment she wanted. However, the experience taught her a valuable lesson about relying on only one form of credit. This situation is fairly common among college graduates who don't have student loans. A lot of graduates will often apply for a credit card to build their credit report, and one into the same problem that Erin Lowry found herself in.

Some credit card companies don't report to all three credit bureaus, which can make it difficult for the cardholder to apply for a loan or rent an apartment. To avoid running into this issue, you should always call your credit card provider to ask if they report to all three credit agencies (Experian, Equifax, and TransUnion). If they don't, then it'll be in your best interest to find a card that does.

A big part of the reason why Lowry ran into this issue in the first place was that she just didn't *know* that her credit card wasn't reporting to all three of the credit bureaus. As a young person who'd just graduated from college, she'd never even heard of the term "thin file," and ultimately just didn't realize how complicated maintaining a good credit score could be. She did ultimately take control of the situation, though, after learning about what she had to do to remedy the issue. You have the power to change your financial situation (and your life as a whole). Just remember that.

In this chapter, I'll delve into the key factors that contribute to good credit. These things are super important to keep in mind, so you may want to bookmark this chapter.

THE KEYS TO GOOD CREDIT

Let's take a look at the five main factors that can affect your credit score below. Once you have a better understanding of how to effectively manage each of these factors, you'll be able to improve your credit score — which should open up the options for your future considerably.

Payment History

Payment history is, without a doubt, the most crucial factor that can impact your credit score. It accounts for about 35% of your overall score, and shows lenders how responsible you are with your credit (i.e. how likely you are to pay your bills on time). Needless to say, late payments or missed payments can hurt your credit score. For example, if you happen to miss a payment on a credit card, it can remain on your credit report for up to seven years.

With this being said, it's very important that you stay on top of your payments no matter what. It may be a good idea to set up payment reminders or automatic payments if you're worried about missing your payment due dates. If you've already missed payments, don't panic. Just try to get caught up as soon as you're able to, and continue to make on-time payments going forward.

Credit Utilization

Your credit utilization accounts for around 30% of your credit score, so it's also a pretty significant factor to keep in mind. As the name suggests, your credit utilization refers to how much of your available credit you're using. High credit utilization may indicate financial instability, which means lenders might not be very keen to approve your loan applications. To paint a picture for you, if you have a credit limit of $10,000 and your outstanding balance is $8,000, your credit utilization would be 80%. This is obviously quite high, and would definitely lower your credit score.

If you want to build better credit, you should try to keep your credit utilization under 30% if you can. If you pay off your balances in full every month, that will help keep your credit utilization low. It may also be a good idea to ask for a credit limit increase to temporarily increase the credit that's available to you. If you're going to do this, though, you'll need to be careful not to overspend.

Length of Credit History

The length of your credit history essentially shows how long you've been using credit and how experienced you are with effectively managing. Your credit history length accounts for 15% of your credit score. In general, the longer your credit history is, the healthier your overall score will be. Young people often wonder how they're supposed to just *automatically* have a long credit history. These things aren't automatic, of course, but it's easier to build up your credit history than you might think.

If you want to build up your credit history, I recommend that you start using credit as soon as possible (while maintaining good credit habits over time, of course). Keeping old credit accounts open can also beef up your credit history, so as long as you're able to keep track of the accounts you're not using anymore, it may be a good idea to keep them open for now.

Credit Mix

Credit mix accounts for about 10% of your credit score, and it refers to the different types of credit accounts you have (i.e. car loans, mortgages, and credit cards). The more diverse your credit mix is, the better your credit score will be. Basically, having an especially diverse credit mix shows lenders that you're good at managing different types of credit responsibly.

If you only have credit card accounts, your credit mix may be pretty limited, which can have a negative impact on your credit score. In order to build up your credit score, you should ideally try to have a diverse mix of different credit accounts. However, you should only take on credit accounts that you can manage responsibly, as you don't want to end up with lines of credit that you can't pay back.

New Credit

New credit also accounts for 10% of your credit score. It shows lenders how frequently you apply for and open new credit accounts. As I mentioned earlier, opening too many new credit accounts in a short period of time generally isn't a good idea. Unfortunately, if you have too many new credit accounts, lenders might think you're financially unstable and reject your loan applications.

In order to build up your credit score, it's always a good idea to be selective when you're opening new credit accounts. You should also only open new accounts when it's absolutely necessary, and you should try to avoid applying for multiple credit accounts at the same time. Applying for, say, five credit cards within one month is a bad idea anyway, as it can be difficult to keep track of your payments for multiple different accounts.

THE 3 BASIC TYPES OF CREDIT

Did you know that credit comes in different forms? This is definitely not something they teach you in school, despite the fact it's important information that everyone should be aware of. Once you gain a basic understanding of the 3 main types of credit, you'll be able to make informed financial decisions and determine the best ways to use each type of credit depending on your situation. Let's take a closer look at the 3 main types of credit below:

Revolving Credit

Revolving credit allows you to borrow money up to a pre-approved credit limit. You can use this type of credit over and over again — as long as you pay off the balance on time. If you have a credit card, you're utilizing revolving credit, just to give you an example. Depending on your credit score and credit history, your credit limit might vary. You may also get charged higher interest rates if you fail to pay off your balance in full every month. Revolving credit typically has no fixed repayment term, and your payment depends on your outstanding balance.

Installment Credit

This type of credit typically involves borrowing a specific amount of money and repaying it over a fixed period (think monthly payments, for example). The most common types of installment credit tend to be personal loans, car loans, student loans, and mortgages. The repayment term can definitely vary. You may have several years or just a few months to pay back an installment credit account. Installment credit usually has a higher credit limit than revolving credit does, and interest rates tend to be lower because the payments are spread out over time.

Open Credit

Open credit allows you to borrow money for a short period of time, usually up to 30 days or so, without any accumulation of interest. With open credit, it's very important that you pay your balance in full before the end of the billing period. Open credit is typically used by businesses to more effectively manage cashflow and purchase necessary inventory. Trade credit and gas cards are both solid examples of open credit. These types of accounts tend to have lower credit limits, but they're oftentimes more flexible.

THE THREE TYPES OF CREDIT

	Revolving Credit	Installment Credit	Open Credit
Credit Limit	Set Limit	Set Limit	Set Limit
Payments	Flexible	Fixed	Flexible
Interest Fees	Yes	Yes	No
Repayment Term	Flexible	Fixed	Flexible

WHY EVERY ADULT SHOULD BE CHECKING THEIR CREDIT SCORE

Again, your credit score is sort of "out-of-sight, out-of-mind" most of the time, and for this reason, it can be difficult to get into the habit of checking it regularly. However, keeping track of your credit score is an absolutely critical aspect of managing your finances. Every adult should be checking their credit score on the regular, and here's why:

Landlords and Employers May Check Your Credit Report

If you've ever applied for an apartment, you know how strict some landlords can be about their tenants' credit scores. A lot of employers tend to be the same way. They want to know that you're reliable and responsible with your money, which is understandable. If you have a low credit score, this could significantly impact your chances of getting hired for your dream job or getting approved for the apartment you've had eyes on for a while now. By checking your credit score regularly, you'll be able to ensure that you're presenting the best possible picture of your creditworthiness.

Mistakes in Credit Report Could Be Negatively Affecting Your Score

Sometimes, credit reports contain errors. This doesn't happen very often, but it's definitely something to be aware of. These errors could be as simple as a misspelled name or incorrect address, or they could be a bit more troublesome. For example, it's crucial to make sure that there aren't any accounts that don't belong to you on your credit report. You should ensure that your credit report isn't listing any missed payments that you actually made on time. If you don't check your credit score regularly, you might not be able to catch these mistakes in a timely manner, which could potentially lead to more problems.

You Could Be Paying More in Interest Than You Need to Be

Interest can certainly build up over time. If you've taken out student loans, you're probably well aware of this fact. Your credit score directly impacts the interest rates you're offered on certain loans and credit cards. If your credit score is on the lower end, you may end up paying a lot more in interest than is ideal. If you regularly monitor your credit score, however, you may be able to qualify for lower interest rates, which could quite literally save you thousands of dollars in the long run.

It's Simply a Matter of Making a Habit of Staying on Top of Your Finances

Although it may sound like a pain, checking your credit score is actually super easy. It only takes a few minutes to review your credit report, and doing so is absolutely worth it. By knowing exactly where you stand with your credit score, you'll be able to make much more informed decisions about borrowing and spending money. Checking your credit score on a regular basis can also help you identify areas where you could improve, such as paying down your debt or making your credit card payments on time.

Credit Mastery Habit #2:

Action Step: Create a personalized action plan based on your unique credit profile.

To establish this habit, you'll want to begin by assessing your current credit utilization rate. Evaluate your payment history and figure out which areas need improvement. From there, you should be able to determine the age of your credit history and review the mix of credit accounts you currently have. Identify any recent credit inquiries that could be having a negative effect on your score, and determine the actions you need to take in order to improve your credit score. Set up a plan for the coming month (I recommend writing this down in a notebook), outlining the steps you'll need to take to improve your score. If you get into the habit of doing this regularly, you shouldn't have any trouble staying on top of your finances.

SEGUE

Building and maintaining a good credit score is totally possible if you're willing to put the time and effort in. It also, of course, helps to be mindful of the different factors that contribute to your credit score. A lot of people don't know where to start when it comes to building credit, but now that you're aware of the keys to good credit (i.e. payment history, credit utilization, length of credit history, credit mix, and new credit), you have a solid foundation to work off of. Remember to check your credit score regularly, as this will help you stay on top of things. It's just another part of being financially responsible! In the next chapter, I'll go over something you've probably been wondering about for a while now: credit cards.

3

CONQUERING CREDIT CARD CHAOS

If you're anything like me, you probably heard nothing but bad things about credit cards growing up. When I was a kid, I remember my friend Ben's parents constantly stressing about money and applying for new credit cards. They, unfortunately, weren't very good about paying off their credit cards in their late twenties and early thirties — which was partly due to the chaos of moving, having kids, and just dealing with the complex events of life in general. Once they finally paid off their debt years later, they warned me, rather excessively, about the dangers of getting a credit card. Ben's dad, on several occasions, advised me not to get a credit card at all, and for most of my twenties, I avoided the temptation to do so.

Now, I'd like to start this chapter off by saying that credit cards are not something that should be feared. You're not giving in to some evil temptation when you decide to apply for a credit card. You're simply doing what you can to build your credit and make a promise to yourself that you're going to be responsible with that credit. I totally understand why Ben's parents didn't want me to ever get a credit card, but I wasn't sure how I was supposed to build significant credit without one. When I told them I was applying for a credit card, his dad said: "That's fine, Kirk, but be responsible. Don't miss any payments, or you'll find yourself falling behind pretty quickly." I took this to heart and eventually learned how to properly manage my credit cards, but not before making a few common mistakes along the way.

Ben's parents and I aren't the only ones who have been through the chaos that sometimes comes with opening up a credit card account. Take the story of Rebecca Lake, for example. Rebecca Lake had a credit card nightmare that was entirely of her own doing. After tying the knot, she made the decision to add her then-spouse to several of her credit card accounts as an authorized user without fully discussing their credit scores or spending habits. Rebecca had hoped that by allowing her partner to use her cards, they could jointly manage their finances and potentially even improve his credit score.

However, this plan backfired pretty much immediately. Her then-spouse went on a spending spree that resulted in over $30,000 in debt on Rebecca's credit cards. Rebecca realized her mistakes (i.e. not discussing money and credit with her partner beforehand and failing to draw solid guidelines on how her credit cards were meant to be used), and, as a result, she was stuck with an enormous debt after her marriage ended.

This experience taught her two important lessons: open communication about money and credit is crucial in any marriage, and adding an authorized user to a credit card should not be taken lightly. It was reading stories like Rebecca's that really got me serious about being a responsible credit card user. Hopefully, her story will give you a bit of inspiration as well. Stories like these show that the main reason so many people end up in debt when they apply for a credit card (or multiple credit cards) is that they simply don't understand how credit cards work.

In this chapter, we'll take a deeper look at how credit cards affect your credit score, as well as the pros and cons of having multiple credit cards. At the end of this section, you'll have the chance to assess your credit card habits and come up with a plan to better optimize your credit card usage.

HOW CREDIT CARDS AFFECT YOUR CREDIT SCORE

As you may already be aware, credit cards can impact your credit score in both positive and negative ways. By applying for a credit card, you can begin to establish a credit history for yourself, which — as previously discussed — is a critical component of your credit score. Having a credit card is, of course, a massive responsibility. If you're able to use your credit card in the way it's meant to be used (i.e. making on-time payments and keeping your balance low) you should see your credit score go up. On the other hand, if you make a lot of late payments or find yourself missing payments altogether, this can hurt your credit score and will demonstrate to lenders that you're maybe not the most responsible borrower.

Opening and closing credit card accounts can impact your credit score as well. When you open a new credit card and increase your overall credit limit, this can lower your credit utilization rate and potentially boost your credit score. However, if you apply for too many credit cards in a short period of time, this essentially lets lenders know that you're taking on too much debt and can lower your credit score. Similarly, when you close a credit card account, this can lower your overall available credit and increase your credit utilization rate, meaning your credit score might take a hit.

In short, credit cards can have a significant impact on your credit score, so it's important to use them responsibly. By making on-time payments, keeping your balance low, and being mindful of your credit utilization rate, you can demonstrate to lenders that you're a responsible borrower and potentially boost your credit score. However, failing to use credit cards responsibly can damage your credit score, so you'll definitely want to be aware of the impact your credit card usage can have on your creditworthiness.

What is the Difference Between Credit and Credit Cards?

If you're confused about the difference between credit and credit cards, you're certainly not alone. While these two things are related, they're definitely distinct concepts. To put it simply, your credit is an overall assessment of your creditworthiness (or ability to pay back the money you've borrowed). You can obtain credit by taking out loans, mortgages, and — most commonly — credit cards. Your credit score shows lenders how responsible you are with borrowed money, and it takes factors like your payment history, credit utilization, and outstanding debts into account.

A credit card, on the other hand, is a specific type of financial product that essentially allows you to borrow money from your bank (or another financial institution). You're required to pay back the amount you borrow *plus* interest fees, typically on a monthly basis. When you use a credit card, the factors that contribute to your credit score can all have a pretty significant impact on your credit score. As I mentioned before, if you're able to make payments on time and keep your credit usage relatively low, you'll likely see an improvement in your credit score. That said, if you carry a high balance or miss a lot of payments, you'll probably see a drop in your credit score. Ultimately, it's all about being responsible and staying on top of things.

UNDERSTANDING CREDIT CARD TERMS AND CONDITIONS

As you can imagine, credit card terms and conditions tend to vary among different credit card issuers. These terms and conditions can have a huge impact on your finances, so it's very important that you have a solid understanding of them before you jump into the process of applying for a credit card. Too many people decide to get a credit card without even reading all of the terms and conditions beforehand, which can obviously lead to some pretty significant issues! This is a bit like adopting a new puppy without doing any research in advance. You don't really know what you're getting yourself into, but the puppy sure is cute. What could possibly go wrong?

A few of the main things that can affect your finances when you get your first credit card are the credit card fees and interest rates that come with it. You'll want to make sure that you understand how these fees and rates work before you apply for a credit card. This includes having a solid grasp of the annual percentage rate (APR), cash advance fees, balance transfer fees, and late payment fees. All of this can add up pretty quickly, so it's a good idea to stay organized and vigilant when it comes to managing your credit cards.

You'll also, of course, want to avoid falling into debt at all costs. You should be able to avoid falling into the dreaded pit of debt pretty easily if you understand the terms and conditions of your credit card. If you end up getting a credit card with high-interest rates and fees, this can make it difficult to pay off your balance in full, which can lead to a cycle of debt. As long as you're aware of the terms and conditions, you should also be able to avoid overspending — which is generally what causes outstanding credit card debt in the first place.

I also recommend taking advantage of any rewards or benefits your credit card issuer offers. Most credit cards offer things like cash back, purchase protections, and even travel rewards. Again, these things will be discussed in the terms and conditions, so it's very important that you read them over carefully. The terms and conditions will also tell you how to redeem these rewards. There's a lot of really helpful information in there! Who knew?

Again, not knowing how credit cards work is one of the main reasons why so many people end up falling into credit card debt. Read all of the terms and conditions, and make a conscious effort to make payments on time, keep your balance low, and avoid damaging your credit score. I know sitting there and reading the terms and conditions might not be the most exciting activity in the world, but it can ultimately save you a whole lot of trouble in the long run.

What About Compound Interest?

Most of the time, your credit card interest will be compounded on a daily basis, which essentially means that your credit card provider charges interest on your account every day (usually based on your average daily balance). Naturally, as your balance increases, the interest added to the amount you owe will also increase. The compounding of interest can result in the accumulation of interest charges fairly quickly and can ultimately increase the cost of carrying a balance on your credit card. If you pay the full statement balance by the due date, however, your credit card issuer won't impose any interest that may have accumulated.

The concept of compound interest refers to when interest is not only charged on the principal amount borrowed or invested but also on the interest that has accumulated. In other words, interest will be added to the initial amount, the sum of which earns more interest over time. While compound interest can work in your favor — especially when it comes to making investments, such as a retirement fund or savings account — it can also work against you if you happen to have accumulated a lot of debt. When interest is compounded on debt (i.e. credit card debt), it can exponentially increase the amount you owe on a particular account.

Let's look at an example, shall we? If you have a credit card balance of $1,000 with an interest rate of, say, 20% compounded daily, the daily interest rate would be 0.0548%. If you don't make any payments for a month, your overall balance would increase to $1,219.50, even though you only borrowed $1,000. The reason for this is that the interest being charged each day is added to your balance, which is then used to calculate the interest for the following day. This is why paying off your credit card balance in full every month is so important. The last thing you want to do is reap the negative effects of compound interest on your debt!

THE PROS AND CONS OF HAVING MULTIPLE CREDIT CARDS

Credit cards can be a useful financial tool when used responsibly, but what happens when you have multiple credit cards? Is having more than one credit card a smart move, or is it a recipe for financial disaster? Well, the fact of the matter is that it can vary depending on your circumstances and situation. Those with multiple credit cards have great purchasing power, more access to rewards, and a backup plan in case of emergencies. That said, having multiple credit cards can oftentimes lead to overspending and high fees, which can cause your debt to pile up pretty quickly.

Let's take a closer look at the pros and cons of having multiple credit cards below. This should help you make an informed decision about whether or not having more than one credit card is a good decision for you personally.

✚ The Pros of Having Multiple Credit Cards

If you're able to handle your finances responsibly (which, of course, is easier said than done), you'll find that there are a lot of advantages to having multiple credit cards. One major benefit of having more than one credit card is that it can impact your credit score in a positive way. Using multiple credit cards can also help to improve your credit utilization. Lenders will see that you're a responsible borrower and will be more inclined to approve you for loans and mortgages should you need them.

Furthermore, if you decide to apply for multiple credit cards (though, ideally, not at the same time as this can indicate financial turmoil), your overall credit limit will increase. This can be particularly useful in emergencies. Please remember to use this increase in credit responsibly, though. Having more credit does not necessarily give you extra room to make frivolous purchases on expensive things that you don't really need. Another benefit of having multiple credit cards is, of course, the ability to take advantage of the different rewards each of your credit cards offers. Use each credit card strategically and responsibly, and you'll be able to earn things like cashback and miles for different types of purchases.

— The Cons of Having Multiple Credit Cards

As you can see, there are plenty of benefits to having multiple credit cards. However, before you start applying for your next credit card, you might want to consider some of the *drawbacks* of having multiple credit cards. One significant concern you'll want to keep in mind is that managing multiple credit cards can be more challenging than most people expect it to be. Keeping track of different due dates, minimum payments, and balances can be extremely overwhelming — which may lead to overspending and the accumulation of debt.

To piggyback off of that, having multiple credit cards will almost certainly increase your risk of accumulating more debt. It may be tempting to use all of your available credit, which can lead to a pile-up of balances that are increasingly difficult to pay off, day by day, due to the interest that accumulates over time. What's more, having multiple credit cards can put your credit score at risk if you don't know how to manage them properly. You've also got to worry about annual fees. Every credit card comes with an annual fee, so the more credit cards you have, the more you'll have to pay in annual fees.

How Many Credit Cards Should You Have?

This is a great question, and the answer really just depends on how many credit cards you're able to effectively manage. For some people, that may be one or two. Others might be able to handle four or five credit cards, but nobody is born knowing how to manage that many at once. As I've already discussed, having more than one credit card is a great way to build credit and earn rewards. It also provides you with a safety net if you happen to find yourself in an emergency situation, which is always a plus.

That said, if you're going to have multiple credit cards, you've got to make sure that you're able to make on-time payments and keep all of your balances low. Having too many credit cards can make it especially challenging to keep track of your various balances and due dates, which means you'll be more at risk of missing payments and, therefore, having to pay late fees. The best approach is to have just enough credit cards — as many as you can manage — to ensure that you can use your credit cards effectively without digging yourself into debt or damaging your credit score.

Tips for Managing Multiple Cards

Managing multiple credit cards can be difficult and honestly takes a lot of practice. I really can't stress this enough. However, I do have some tips to offer you if you struggle to stay on top of your finances and are considering applying for multiple credit cards. Again, do not apply for multiple cards at the same time! I know you know this, but it's super important, so I'll do what I can to drive the point home.

I recommend getting a calendar or planner so that you can effectively keep track of all of the payment due dates for each of your credit cards. It's easy to make mistakes and miss payments, so you'll want to do what you can to stay on top of everything. Many credit card issuers actually offer online tools that can help you manage your accounts and track your spending. You can even set up automatic alerts for your due dates so that you never miss a payment. I also recommend setting up autopay, as this will allow you to make on-time payments every month without even having to think about it that much. If you set up autopay, however, you'll want to review your statements regularly so that you're aware of any changes in interest rates or fees for your credit cards.

When you have multiple credit cards, it's a good idea to make sure that you're using all of the benefits properly as well. Depending on the types of purchases you make with your cards, different cards will offer different rewards (i.e. cashback or points). If you have specific cards for specific types of purchases, this will help you maximize your rewards (and save money, too). Managing multiple credit cards is likely going to take a bit of trial and error, but once you learn how to use your credit cards responsibly and strategically, you'll be able to improve your credit score as well as your overall financial health.

CREDIT CARD UTILIZATION: THE SWEET SPOT

Using a credit card responsibly is all about finding a good balance — the sweet spot, if you will — of credit card utilization. Naturally, this may require some slight lifestyle changes and fine-tuning. As I discussed previously, your credit card utilization measures how much of your available credit limit you're using. Calculating your credit card utilization is a fairly simple process. Just divide your credit balance by your credit limit and multiply by 100. For example, if you have a credit card balance of $500 and your credit limit is $2,000, your credit card utilization would be 25%.

When it comes to credit card utilization, there are some basic rules of thumb you'll want to keep in mind. Ideally, you should aim to use less than 30% of your credit limit on each of your cards. This means that if you have a credit limit of $10,000, for example, you should try to keep your balance below $3,000. That said, if you need to make a large purchase that happens to exceed your credit limit, it's okay to go over the recommended utilization rate. Just make sure to pay it off as soon as possible so that you're not carrying around a high balance for too long.

You should try to keep your utilization rate low over the long term, as a high utilization rate can negatively affect your credit score. It's also important to take note of the difference between per-card utilization and total utilization. In short, per-card utilization measures how much of each card's credit limit you're using, while total utilization — as the name suggests — measures how much of your overall credit limit you're using across *all* of your cards. As long as you're able to keep your credit card utilization in the sweet spot, you should see your credit score improve significantly.

HOW TO USE CREDIT CARDS TO BUILD CREDIT

"So, how can I use my credit cards to actually build credit?" If you're asking this question, you're not the only one. Strategically using your credit cards to build up your credit can admittedly be a bit confusing. Take it one step at a time, though, and you'll eventually find that managing your credit cards (and using them in such a way that your credit score goes up) is not so overwhelming after all. Let's take a closer look at the ways in which you can use your credit cards to build credit below:

Use Only the Credit You Need

This means not using your credit cards to make frivolous purchases. In other words, try to refrain from buying things that you can't really afford. It's important to remember that credit cards are not a substitute for income, and, therefore, you should only use your credit card when you absolutely need to. If you use your credit card to buy only what you need and can afford, you'll be able to ensure that you can pay that money back in time, which will help you establish a positive credit history.

Pay off Balances in Full

Paying off your credit card balance in full every month is another great way to establish a good credit history. You'll also be able to avoid carrying a balance that could accumulate interest charges, which can add up rather quickly over time. If you consistently make on-time payments, this will show lenders that you're responsible with credit; and once you've made enough on-time payments, you should see your credit score start to go up.

Monitor Your Transaction History

Regularly reviewing your credit card transaction history is honestly one of the best things you can do for yourself. It's always a good idea to make sure that all of the charges on your account are legitimate and accurate. This will help you avoid becoming a victim of fraud, as well as ensure that you're only paying for the charges that you actually made. If you notice any errors or charges that you didn't make in your transaction history, make sure to report them to your credit card issuer immediately.

Track Your Overall Credit

If you want to build your credit over time, I recommend keeping constant tabs on your credit score and credit report. You'll have an easier time identifying areas for improvement when you check your credit score regularly. You'll also be able to get a visual representation of how your credit changes over time. Remember: you can get a free credit report from any of the three major credit bureaus once a year.

Pick the Right Credit Card

This is a little known fact, but choosing the right credit card can make a huge difference when it comes to your ability to build credit. Look for cards that offer rewards for responsible credit behavior, and be sure to consider the fees associated with each card you decide to apply for. Some credit cards offer credit limit increases over time, which can help improve your credit utilization ratio, so that's definitely something to keep in mind as well.

HOW TO AVOID COMMON CREDIT CARD MISTAKES

If you don't know how to use your credit card wisely, you could end up in serious financial trouble. Don't worry, though, because it's actually pretty easy to avoid the most common credit card mistakes people run into. One of the most common mistakes people make is paying only the minimum amount on their credit cards each month. This can result in high-interest charges, which can lead to a vicious cycle of debt that's very difficult to escape. In order to keep this from happening, make sure to pay off your balance in full every month — or, at the very least, pay more than the minimum amount.

Another mistake people make is missing payments altogether. This can lead to things like late fees and penalty interest rates, which can negatively impact your credit score. To avoid missing payments, you should definitely set up automatic payments or reminders so that you don't forget to pay on time every month. Make sure to read the terms and conditions of each of your credit cards, as this will help you better understand how the applicable fees and interest rates actually work.

Taking out cash advances is another common costly mistake people make. It's important to keep in mind that cash advances typically come with high-interest rates and fees, and this interest starts accruing immediately. In general, you should try to avoid taking out cash advances altogether unless it's an emergency and you have absolutely no other options.

Applying for new credit cards too often can hurt your credit score as well. Every time you apply for a new credit card, it will be considered a hard inquiry on your credit report, and hard inquiries, unfortunately, lower your credit score. I recommend only applying for new credit cards when you need them and can afford to manage them responsibly. This will help you avoid overspending and digging yourself into more debt.

Closing a credit card can also have a negative impact on your credit score. When you close a credit card, it reduces your available credit, which, in turn, increases your credit utilization rate. Unfortunately, if you have a high credit utilization rate, your credit score is likely to take a hit. If you want to close one of your credit cards, make sure to pay off the balance first and consider keeping the card open if it doesn't have a significant annual fee attached to it.

Credit Mastery Habit #3:

Action Step: Assess your credit card habits and devise a plan to optimize your credit card usage.

The first thing you'll want to do is evaluate your current credit card balances and interest rates. From there, you should be able to determine which cards are costing you the most money and prioritize paying off those balances first. Next, evaluate your credit card usage and determine which areas you can improve upon. This may include cutting or reducing unnecessary spending or finding ways to increase your income. After you figure out which credit cards you want to keep, create a payment plan to pay down your balances. Use your credit cards responsibly going forward. I recommend writing out a plan for the upcoming month that includes making on-time payments and using your credit cards for essential purchases only.

SEGUE

Applying for a credit card (or multiple credit cards) is not a decision that should be taken lightly. It's very important that you understand all of the terms and conditions that come with getting a credit card so that you don't end up in a situation where you're surprised by things like accumulated interest or late payment fees. It's always a good idea to make your monthly payments on time, as this will help you avoid having to pay extra fees. Paying on time will also improve your credit score, so it's definitely worth it. In the next chapter, I'll discuss some strategies for paying off debt. When it comes to demolishing debt, you need to have a plan. Why not come up with that plan today?

4

DEBT DEMOLITION: THE ULTIMATE BATTLE PLAN

Did you know that the average American owes over $96,000 in debt? I'm not sharing this statistic to scare you — it's simply a harrowing truth. In today's economic climate, staying out of debt is no easy task. A lot of Americans have to take on debt to be able to make ends meet, which is in part due to high-interest rates and the high cost of living. The fact that so many people owe so much debt also has to do with the average American's inherent inability to efficiently plan how they're going to pay back all of the debt they owe. Debt is vicious. It accumulates fast, and if you're not regularly checking up on it and making payments, you're more than likely to find yourself in a whole lot more debt than you originally started with.

To put it plainly, this... stinks. What you need to know now is how to dig yourself *out* of that accumulated debt. Allow me to share a story with you about my good friend, Sophie. Sophie is a 36-year-old single mother of two who unfortunately found herself buried in debt after going through a divorce and several unexpected expenses. She had credit card debt, a car loan, and student loans — all of which added up to a whopping $60,000 or so. Needless to say, she felt stressed and overwhelmed. She developed some pretty unhealthy coping mechanisms, like drinking too much and spending a lot of time in bed, which ultimately made things worse.

Eventually, Sophie realized that she had to take control of her finances and dig herself out of debt. The only problem was she didn't know how to do this. In fact, she wasn't sure where to even start. After doing some research and meeting with a financial consultant, Sophie was able to come up with a plan. The first thing she did was create a budget, which meant cutting back on expenses like alcohol and junk food and allocating more money toward her debt payments. She decided to pay off the debts with the highest interest rates first, which alleviated a lot of her stress.

She also took on extra work in order to increase her income and put more money towards her debt.

Needless to say, working a 9-5 shift at her office and then going to work *another* shift at the diner next door wasn't ideal — but it did help Sophie pay off her debt a lot faster. Although it was difficult, she stuck to her plan and eventually started to see results. She celebrated small victories and stayed motivated by reminding herself of how being debt-free would give her the ability to save for her children's education (as well as plan for her own retirement).

After five years of hard work and dedication, Sophie paid off all of her debts. For the first time in forever, she felt free and was proud of herself for putting in all that effort to pay everything off. Now that she's debt-free, she's been able to focus more on improving her kids' lives and saving for their futures. Her story, I believe, is a great demonstration of the difference that hard work, determination, and a solid plan can make to those who are buried in debt. Digging yourself out of debt isn't easy. Sophie would tell you firsthand that it takes an incredible amount of patience and persistence, but the reward of financial freedom and peace of mind is well worth it.

In this chapter, I'll discuss some strategies you can use to reduce and eventually pay off your debt. I'll delve into the difference between good debt and bad debt, as well as how you can begin to go about creating a budget, prioritizing your payments, and consolidating your debt. It's essentially all about making your debt work for you rather than against you, and I'd like to provide you with practical advice on how to do exactly this. Whether you're dealing with debt or are looking to take out debt in the future, my aim with this section is to offer you valuable insights into making informed financial decisions that can help you avoid the burden of debt. Let's get started, shall we?

UNDERSTANDING THE TYPES OF DEBT

Debt is not a particularly well-understood concept. People dislike it — and for good reason — but that also means they don't talk about it enough. When it comes to evaluating your debt, it's crucial that you're able to establish flexible guidelines for what constitutes good or bad debt. Categorizing debt isn't necessarily a matter of black and white or good or bad, but it could benefit you to determine a general rule of thumb for what qualifies as "good debt" in theory.

Good debt typically refers to debt that you've incurred for a particular asset, which is expected to appreciate in value or offer increased value in the future. When you take out a mortgage for your home or take out a loan for real estate, you're accumulating good debt. That said, the parameters for determining what qualifies as good debt should be defined rather loosely.

For instance, if you take out a mortgage on your home, this is considered good debt because your home will appreciate in value over time. Similarly, if you take out a loan for real estate, it will provide you with appreciation, depreciation, and income and — in turn — allowing your money to work for you. The thing about accumulating good debt is that you'll be walking a fine line, no matter what kind of debt you decide to take out. You still have to be responsible.

If you acquire excessive mortgage debt on your home, and it becomes too much to manage, this good debt can turn into bad debt pretty quickly. If you run the numbers well for your piece of real estate on the front end and there are a lot of costly repairs, that good debt could turn into bad debt as well. In general, it's important to keep in mind that not all debt is created equal, and even debt that's considered "good" can become bad if taken out in excess.

THE DIFFERENCES BETWEEN GOOD AND BAD DEBT

Referring to debt as either "good" or "bad" is honestly a bit vague, so it makes sense that most people find it confusing. In general, good debt is considered to be an investment in your future financial well-being, whereas bad debt can hinder your financial health in the long run. It's important to be aware of the different types of debt and the potential consequences associated with them before you make any important financial decisions. Let's take a closer look at some examples of good and bad debt below.

✚ *Examples of Good Debt*

Mortgage

A mortgage is the type of loan most people take out when they want to purchase a home. Mortgage debt is typically considered to be good debt since it allows you to own a valuable asset (i.e. a home), which will increase in value over several years. Making mortgage payments can also help build equity, which you can then use to finance your future.

Home Equity Loan

When you've built up a certain amount of equity in your home, you might want to take out a home equity loan. Most people use home equity loans for things like home improvements and debt consolidation. Home equity loans are considered to be a good type of debt because they come with lower interest rates.

Line of Credit

A line of credit is like a flexible loan that lets you borrow money up to a certain limit set by your credit card company. This type of loan is considered to be good debt because you can use it to fund investments in things like a small business, which could potentially pay off and help you earn money in the future.

Student Loan

This one is a bit controversial, but most people who attend college end up taking out student loans at one point or another. Student loans can be considered good debt because you're using them to fund your education, but you need to be wise and not max out your student loans to live. Even though the greatest return you can ever receive is investing in yourself, student loans can get out of hand and become bad debt as well.

Small Business Loan

If you're planning on starting a new business (or trying to expand an existing one), you might want to take out a small business loan to help fund it. Small business loans are considered to be a good type of debt, as they can help you grow your business and your wealth. Like student loans, small business loans can be an excellent investment.

— *Examples of Bad Debt*

Credit Cards

Credit cards allow you to borrow money for things like emergency situations and big purchases, but they tend to come with high-interest rates and can lead you to fall into the cycle of debt if you don't use them responsibly. Credit card debt is considered to be bad debt since it's often used to finance non-essential things that don't generate any income.

Payday Loans

Payday loans are short-term, high-interest loans that people typically take out when they need to cover immediate expenses. These loans tend to come with extremely high-interest rates, which means you're likely to end up in more debt if you decide to take one out. Payday loans are considered to be a bad type of debt because they can have devastating long-term financial consequences.

Car Loans

Most people end up needing to take out a car loan at some point. After all, it's pretty hard to function, in this day and age, without a car. Some may argue that this type of debt is necessary, but car loans are generally considered to be bad debt because cars depreciate (i.e. lose value) over time.

THE IMPACT OF DEBT ON YOUR CREDIT SCORE

The debt you carry is a huge part of your financial life as a whole. It can have a major impact on your spending ability, your credit score, and your capacity to get low insurance rates or borrow money. Your credit score depends heavily on how much debt you happen to carry. In fact, your debt accounts for about 30% of your credit score, so it's definitely not something you want to brush aside. This calculation takes your credit utilization into account (which, again, is the ratio of your credit card balance to your credit limit).

When your credit card balances get too high, your credit score suffers — especially if your cards are maxed out or go over the limit. Even if your debt-to-income ratio is relatively low, you could still be denied for things like new credit cards and car loans if you have a bad credit score. You can thankfully improve your score by paying off your loan balances, but this is oftentimes a slow process, especially if your loans come with high-interest rates.

How you choose to manage your debt has a direct impact on your credit score. If you pay off your balances quickly, you can increase your credit score by lowering your credit utilization. However, if you have too much debt and can't keep up with payments, your credit score will suffer. Missing payments can lower your credit score, so it's important that you manage your debt effectively. If you choose to request a debt settlement or file for bankruptcy, it can negatively impact your credit score for months or even years — so you should probably only consider doing this as a last resort.

Some people who have low credit scores choose to go to credit counseling. Credit counseling itself won't hurt your credit score, but the debt consolidation process might. Opening a new account can lower your average credit age, which accounts for 15% of your credit score. While some debt solutions can harm your credit score, they may still be worth considering. In the long run, credit counseling and debt consolidation could be very helpful since these things tend to make it easier for people to pay off their debt in full.

THE DEBT-TO-INCOME RATIO

Perhaps you've heard of the term "debt-to-income ratio" before, but what does this actually mean? In short, your debt-to-income (DTI) ratio is a financial measurement of how much of your monthly income goes toward paying off your debts. Banks and lenders use this ratio to determine whether or not you're able to take on new debt while also paying back existing loans. If you have a high DTI ratio, this might suggest to lenders that you have difficulty paying back loans, which means you may get charged high-interest rates or be denied loans altogether.

Most people don't know what their debt-to-income ratio is right off the bat. To calculate your DTI ratio, the first thing you'll want to do is add up all of your monthly debt payments (i.e. your rent or mortgage payment, your car loans, your credit card payments, and your student loans). From there, divide this total number by your gross monthly income before taxes. Then, finally, multiply *this* number by 100 to get your DTI ratio as a percentage.

For example, let's say your total monthly debt payments add up to $1,500, and your gross monthly income is $4,000. Your DTI ratio calculation would look like this:

$$(\$1{,}500 / \$4{,}000) \times 100 = 37.5\%$$

A DTI ratio of 43% or lower is generally considered to be good, as it indicates that you have a manageable amount of debt relative to your income. If you have a DTI ratio that's above 43%, you may have difficulty getting approved for new loans, as it suggests that you struggle to make your monthly payments. While your DTI ratio doesn't directly affect your credit score, banks and lenders will still want to look at this ratio when they're assessing your creditworthiness. As long as you're able to maintain a low DTI ratio, you shouldn't have any trouble getting approved for new loans or credit cards should you need them.

Debt-to-Income Vs Debt-to-Credit Ratios

Debt-to-credit and DTI ratios are similar, but it's important that you don't get them mixed up. Your debt-to-credit ratio is the amount you owe on all revolving credit accounts compared to the amount of credit that's available to you. Depending on the credit scoring model being used, your debt-to-credit ratio may be a factor in calculating your credit score.

Your DTI ratio, on the other hand, is the total amount of debt you have each month in comparison to your monthly income. This ratio doesn't impact your credit score, though — once again — lenders will typically take a gander at it when deciding whether or not to approve you for additional credit.

STRATEGIES FOR PAYING OFF DEBT

So, what can you do to actually go about paying off your debts? If you've ever tried to pay off your debts, you're probably aware that it's easier said than done. It takes more time and patience than most people think it will, so it's important that you keep that in mind and stay vigilant when it comes to saving, budgeting, and making debt payments.

One of the best ways to get ahead of your debts is to make payments more than once per month. This can help reduce the amount of interest you'll have to pay over time, as well as help you stay on track with your monthly bills. It's also a good idea to pay more than the minimum amount each month if you're able to. You might need to alter some of your spending habits, but it will definitely be worth it since you'll be paying off your debt a lot faster.

I would also recommend keeping track of your different bills and due dates. There's nothing worse than having to pay a late fee because you simply *forgot* to pay a bill on time. If you're struggling to make ends meet, you may want to consider trading in your car for a more affordable option. This isn't particularly ideal, but it can help reduce your monthly expenses and free up some extra cash for debt repayment.

Cutting costs is never fun, but it may be necessary to do so if you want to be efficient and vigilant in paying off your debts. Start by looking at your grocery spending and see if there are any areas where you can cut back. If groceries take up a significant portion of your weekly spending, you might want to consider being strategic with what you are purchasing.

If you're still struggling to make debt payments, you might want to consider getting a second job or a side gig to bring in some extra income. Setting up a proper budget and tracking your spending habits can also be quite helpful, as can canceling unnecessary monthly subscriptions to services like Netflix and Amazon Prime. It may also be a good idea to talk to a financial advisor or debt counselor. They should be able to provide you with some much-needed guidance.

The Debt Avalanche and Debt Snowball Methods

If you've accumulated a lot of debt over time, you might need to use an even more strategic approach to pay all of it off. The debt avalanche and debt snowball methods are two extremely popular strategies people use for paying off debt. The avalanche method involves paying off your balance with the highest interest rate first, which is what my friend, Sophie, did. The snowball method works the opposite way (i.e. you pay off your smallest debts first and work your way up).

The avalanche method is designed to minimize the amount of interest you're required to pay over time. By taking care of the debt with the highest interest rate first, you'll be putting more money toward paying off the principal amount of debt. This method is especially ideal for people who have a good handle on their finances. It's generally a great way to get out of debt in a shorter amount of time while also saving money in the long run. That said, this method requires a whole lot of discipline and commitment, and you'll definitely want to have a steady income as well.

The snowball method is designed to build momentum and motivation, as you'll be paying off your smaller debts first. A lot of people who use this method feel a sense of accomplishment as they pay off their small debts quickly, which may inspire them to start paying off their larger debts. However, those who use this method tend to acquire more interest on their debts over time since they aren't taking care of their higher-interest debts first. The snowball method also tends to be more affordable in the short term — though utilizing this method can make it take longer to pay off all of your debts.

THE IMPORTANCE OF AVOIDING NEW DEBT

It can be difficult to avoid taking on debt. More often than not, it's a necessary step when it comes to reaching new milestones and achieving your life goals. That said, debt can be an extremely heavy burden to bear, so it's generally a good idea to avoid taking on any new debt if at all possible.

Avoiding new debt will give you a lot more flexibility, both financially and in life in general. Without the burden of monthly payments and interest charges weighing you down, you'll have more resources at your disposal to pursue your life goals — as well as new career opportunities. You'll also be able to save money for your future, which your future self will definitely thank you for.

If you're able to avoid new debt, you'll have a much easier time building the habits that will help you improve your credit score. By paying off your existing debts and not taking on any new debt, you'll be able to show lenders that you're a responsible borrower as well as build a positive credit history. Again, it's all about building a better future for yourself. Too many people are still paying off their debts when they're in their 60s and 70s, so I recommend that you start doing what you can to pay off your debts now while you're still young.

Credit Mastery Habit #4:

Action Step: Design a customized debt repayment plan that aligns with your financial goals.

The first thing you'll want to do is review all of your current debts, along with their interest rates. List all of your debts — including loans and credit cards — and organize them based on their interest rates. The next thing you'll want to do is evaluate your monthly budget and figure out how much money you'll be able to allocate to debt repayment. After that, you'll need to decide which debt repayment strategy will work best for you (i.e. avalanche or snowball method). The strategy you decide to use will generally depend on your current financial situation. Once you've figured that out, set a timeline for paying off all of your debts. Try to break it down into monthly goals and track your progress along the way. I recommend using a debt repayment plan spreadsheet or app to help you stay motivated and organized throughout this process.

SEGUE

If you feel like you're buried in a pit of debt, you're not the only one. Although it may feel insurmountable, paying off your debt is entirely possible if you know what strategies to use. It's also crucial that you're willing to put the effort in and accept that paying off your debts will take time. Don't worry, though, because once you pay off all of your debts, you'll have a lot more financial freedom — and that's definitely worth fighting for. In the next chapter, I'll discuss some critical credit repair techniques, including how to rebuild damaged credit and negotiate with creditors.

CREDIT REPAIR: THE ART OF BOUNCING BACK

If you have a low credit score, you might feel like it's already too late for you to try to get it back up. You probably already know what I'm going to say here: it's never too late to start building your credit score back up, even if your score is in the low 500s. Take this story about a young man that Virginia Coffee — the Branch Manager of Citizens Bank in Avon — worked with a couple of years ago. She had already been working with this particular customer for quite a long time and wanted to do everything she could to help him improve his credit score, which left a lot to be desired.

This young man was, unfortunately, pretty clueless about managing his finances. He was working for a not-the-most-stable employer in the world and was constantly worrying about being able to cash his paychecks. He found himself stuck in a financial rut — living paycheck to paycheck while also attempting to live outside of his means — which is why he went to Virginia for help. "I want to have a car and a home at some point," he told her. "I want to be able to move up in life."

Although the situation was complicated, Virginia didn't give up on him. She knew that he had at least enough money to take out a secured loan, which is a type of loan that's generally reserved for people who want to build their credit. He ended up taking out a couple of secured loans, which slowly helped him build his credit. Eventually, he was able to qualify for a car loan, which Virginia helped him out with. It was a very proud moment for both of them, but unfortunately, things fell apart soon after that.

He ended up losing both his parents and his girlfriend in a freak accident and was obviously devastated after the fact. His financial life took a major hit, as he was responsible for organizing the funeral services for his loved ones. During this time, he fell behind on his credit card payments and watched his credit score drop once more. Understandably, he had a very hard time keeping track of his finances while attempting to cope with this tragedy, and Virginia saw that. She stayed in close contact with him and did what she could to help him get back on track, urging him to keep his employment stable so that he could continue to pay off his loans and credit card payments.

Just the other week, he sent Virginia a text. *"I think I'm ready,"* he said. *"I want to see what I need to do to buy a house."* Virginia couldn't help but tear up a little. "We've come a long way together," she said, looking back over their 10-year-long relationship. "You really put the work in, and now you've reached your goal." Needless to say, she was incredibly proud of how far this young man had come, especially considering all that he'd been through.

Virginia has some advice for anyone who's in a similar spot: find a banker you trust who truly has your best interests at heart. They'll be able to educate you and help you out with things like taking out loans, getting a mortgage, making investments, and — of course — building your credit. The journey to financial well-being is oftentimes a long and arduous one, but you'll get there, especially if you have somebody you can depend on to help you along the way. For many people, money is an extremely personal matter. Trust me, I get it. However, even if you feel embarrassed about your credit score (as I once did), you don't have to go through this journey alone. There are people who are literally there to help you, and although it may take some time, you should be able to build up your credit and eventually achieve your financial goals — just like Virginia's long-term customer did.

In this chapter, we'll be taking a closer look at some common causes of bad credit. I'll also be going over how to identify errors on your credit report, as they can be difficult to spot if you don't know what to look for. Lastly, I'll be delving into the intricacies of negotiating with creditors and the pros and cons of hiring a credit repair service. By the end of this section, you'll know how to pick out any inaccuracies on your credit report and initiate disputes — which will be a very important step in getting your credit score up. Let's jump right in!

COMMON CAUSES OF BAD CREDIT

If you've ever checked your credit report and wondered: "Wait… why is my score so low?" you're definitely not the only one. There are a lot of different reasons why your credit score might be suffering. Many people have low scores because they simply don't understand what's damaging their credit in the first place. Let's take a look at some of the most common causes of bad credit so that you can better understand the factors that may be affecting your score.

Neglecting Bills

When you can't afford to pay your bills, it can be tempting to ignore them altogether — especially if you'd rather spend that money on a brand new pair of shoes or the upcoming *Zelda* game. Some people believe that if they wait long enough, their credit card or mortgage company will simply "give up" and write off their debt. However, a lot of people don't know that when a lender writes off a debt, it becomes a big black mark on their credit report. Your lender might also send your debt to a collection agency, and the credit bureaus will be informed of this.

Your credit score will almost certainly take a hit if you decide to neglect your bills, however, this problem is fixable. If you have a seriously overdue bill, it's important that you take action right away. Don't wait for the creditor to give up. Call them and ask what you need to do to catch up on your payments, and if a particular bill has already gone to collections, see if the creditor will call the account back so that you can pay them directly. If not, you'll need to work with the collection agency to resolve your debt. Remember, the longer you wait, the more damage your unpaid bills will do to your credit score, so you'll want to address this issue as soon as you can.

Not Paying Current Bills First

Naturally, if one of your bills goes to collections, you'll be eager to deal with it right away. However, if you put too much focus on your bills that have gone to collections, you might end up neglecting your other bills — which will only cause more issues and further damage your credit score. Of course, it's super important to pay off your collections account, and you should do so as soon as you're able to, but what a lot of people don't realize is that it's equally important to make sure you're not neglecting your other bills in the process. If you miss payments on other accounts while paying off your collections account, you'll only be creating more problems for yourself.

To avoid this issue, you're going to want to learn how to prioritize your payments correctly. I recommend starting by paying the minimum amount that's due on your current bills. From there, you can use your remaining funds to pay off your collection accounts. Yes, it might take a little bit longer to pay off your debt, but you'll be a lot less likely to accumulate more debt over time. Keep in mind that collection agencies can be *very* persistent. They're trying to put pressure on you to make payments as soon as possible, but you shouldn't be tempted to put all of your focus on paying them off if you've got other bills you should pay off first.

Filing for Bankruptcy

When you file for bankruptcy, you're essentially admitting that you're unable to meet your financial obligations and need to resort to legal measures to be able to resolve your debt. Don't get me wrong — filing for bankruptcy is completely necessary in some (incredibly drastic) situations, but it shouldn't be your go-to solution. Because filing for bankruptcy indicates financial hardship and poor credit utilization, it can severely impact your credit score. That said, if you've gone through bankruptcy, there are still steps you can take to improve your score after the fact.

For example, by paying your bills on time, managing your credit card usage in a responsible way, and regularly checking your credit report, you should be able to rebuild your credit score. Of course, this will be a very gradual process, and it's going to take a lot of grit and determination. You might need to change some of your spending habits and live below your means for a bit while playing catch-up. It'll absolutely be worth it, though, to get back on track and restore your financial health.

Maxing Out Your Credit Cards

It's no wonder that most people have a hard time understanding how credit works. In order to build a healthy credit score, you must use credit; however, if you use it excessively, it can damage your credit utilization ratio and ultimately hurt your score. It's quite the paradox! As I mentioned before, your credit utilization ratio makes up about 30% of your credit score, and even the smallest increase can end up affecting your rating in a negative way. You'll need to figure out a way to maintain a good balance so that your credit utilization ratio remains healthy.

Once again, this comes down to responsible spending and not making any purchases that you know you won't be able to pay back in a timely manner. Avoid overusing your credit card (it's more addicting than you might think!) and strike a balance that helps you maintain a strong credit rating. This will show lenders that you're responsible with credit, which means you'll be more likely to get accepted for new credit cards and loans — should you need them.

Applying for Credit Too Often

I've briefly gone over this already, but it's worth reiterating. Every time you apply for a credit card or personal loan, the lender will typically run a hard credit inquiry to assess your creditworthiness. Every time someone runs a hard credit inquiry, your credit score takes a hit. This is especially true if you've accumulated too many hard inquiries within a short period of time. This is one of the main reasons why people end up with really low credit scores. Credit cards and loans can be awfully nice when it comes to managing certain expenses, but it's very easy to get addicted to overspending. If you're constantly overspending, you're going to feel like you need more credit — hence the vicious cycle of applying for credit too often but not getting approved for good credit because your score is too low.

If you've recently applied for a loan or credit card, I would highly recommend that you refrain from submitting any more applications for the time being — especially if you have a limited credit history. Instead, you should try to focus on cutting any unnecessary expenses and living within your means. Credit is a very powerful tool, and it's important to keep that in mind. What did Uncle Ben say in the first Toby Maguire *Spider-Man* movie? Oh, yeah. "With great power comes great responsibility." So true, Uncle Ben. So true.

HOW TO SPOT ERRORS AND INACCURACIES ON YOUR CREDIT REPORT

By now, you're probably well aware of just how critical checking your credit report on the regular is to your overall financial well-being. As I mentioned before, your credit report provides an overview of your credit history, which lenders use to determine your creditworthiness. Unfortunately, however, credit reports can contain — *pause for horror movie sound effects* — significant errors and inaccuracies that can harm your credit score and even ruin your chances of obtaining more credit. This is why reviewing your credit report regularly is so important. If there are any errors that are impacting your credit score, you're going to want to do what you can to correct them as soon as possible. Let's take a closer look at some of the types of errors and inaccuracies you should keep an eye out for while reviewing your credit report below.

Identity Errors

This is the most common type of credit report error. Perhaps your name is spelled incorrectly, or your report lists an address or social security number that's different from your own. Identity errors tend to be born from typos and data entry mistakes — simple accidents that are thankfully very easy to fix. Sometimes, however, identity errors can happen if you're a victim of identity theft or fraud. This can lower your credit score pretty significantly, so it's important to take care of these errors and figure out what's causing them immediately upon discovering them.

Account Status Errors

Your credit score might take a hit if your account's status is incorrect or outdated for whatever reason. Perhaps you've paid off your account, but it's still listed as delinquent on your credit report, and this is impacting your score. Make sure to keep an eye out for account status errors, as they can give lenders an inaccurate impression of your creditworthiness. It shouldn't be too difficult to keep your account's status up-to-date. Just be vigilant, and, as always, check your credit report often!

Data Management Errors

Data management errors tend to happen when information from one account accidentally gets applied to another, or when certain accounts are merged incorrectly. If you find that someone else's account information is showing up on your credit report, for example, it's likely due to a data management error. This type of error can be tricky to fix, and it may take some time to get it resolved. Still, though, it's a good idea to address data management errors as soon as you find them on your report.

Balance Errors

If the balance on your credit report is showing as incorrect, it's likely due to a balance error (as the name suggests). Your account might show that your balance is higher than what you actually owe, for example. This can be frustrating, as balance errors can make it seem like you're not responsible with your credit, and lenders might deny your credit card or loan applications because of this. There's nothing worse than when your credit score takes a dive for no real reason, so, to avoid this, you should always make sure that your account balances are accurate.

HOW TO DISPUTE ERRORS ON YOUR CREDIT REPORT

So, you've found a few errors on your credit report. I know how frustrating that can be, and if you're anything like I was in my mid-twenties, you probably don't know much about how to dispute these errors.

That's okay because I've learned a lot over the years, and I'm here to pass on that knowledge to you now. Disputing errors on your credit report can be an awfully time-consuming process, but it's incredibly necessary. If you ignore any errors or inaccuracies on your credit report, your credit score is only going to get worse and worse, so although it may take a long time, the disputing process is definitely worth going through.

The first thing you'll need to do is send a letter to the credit bureau that generated the report with the errors you're disputing. In this letter, you should include a detailed explanation of the errors you've discovered, as well as supporting documentation of these errors — such as blank statements or canceled checks. You'll also want to keep a copy of this letter and all of your supporting documentation for your records.

Next, you should determine whether or not you need to contact the specific creditor. If the error you're disputing is related to a particular account, you may want to contact that creditor directly to see what happened. In some cases, the creditor may be able to resolve the issue faster than the credit bureau. This is honestly great, because things of a bureaucratic nature tend to take *forever*.

After sending your dispute letter to the credit bureau, you'll need to wait 45 days for them to respond. I know,

I know. Why does it take *so long*? Unfortunately, that's bureaucracy for you. If their investigation takes longer than this, they're required to inform you of the reason for the delay and provide you with an estimated date for when they'll actually complete your case. Once you finally receive a response, take some time to go over the results of the credit bureau's investigation. If the bureau determines that the error you're disputing is valid, they'll remove it from your credit report. If not, they'll be required to give you a written explanation of why they believe the information is accurate.

Once your dispute has been resolved (in one way or another), you should keep checking your credit report for updates. Make sure that the error has been removed and that your credit report is completely correct. Sending a dispute letter and waiting for a month and a half certainly isn't fun, but you'll ultimately thank yourself for going through this process later. Some credit bureaus might offer you the option to dispute errors online, but that really depends. Before disputing any errors online, you'll definitely want to look over the bureau's specific policies.

HOW TO NEGOTIATE WITH CREDITORS

Did you know that you can negotiate with creditors? I sure didn't when I was dealing with the worst of my credit issues! The idea of negotiating with creditors might be a bit daunting. Effective negotiating essentially takes practice, but I do have some tips you might want to take a look at to help you get started.

First and foremost, you should figure out whether or not you should even negotiate in the first place. If you're struggling with debt, negotiating with your creditors can be a great way to work out a repayment plan that's more manageable for you. However, if you're unable to make any payments at all, most creditors aren't going to take your negotiation attempts seriously. You may also want to do some research into your rights beforehand. When dealing with creditors, know that they're not allowed to harass you or use abusive language. You also have the right to dispute any debts you believe to be incorrect — don't let anyone tell you otherwise.

Before negotiating with your creditors, you should make sure that you have a clear understanding of your financial situation. They're a lot more likely to take your negotiations into account if you're able to provide them with your income, your living expenses, and your various debt obligations. It's not a bad idea to practice what you're going to say in the mirror beforehand, just to ensure that you really know what you're talking about and won't stumble over your words. You should also, of course, get all of your records together. If you're able to present your creditors with relevant bills, bank statements, receipts, and so on, it'll help your case significantly.

I would also recommend taking notes while negotiating. Keep a clear record of all the conversations you have with your creditors, including dates, times, and names. This will help you keep track of any agreements made and serve as solid proof that you've gone through the negotiation process. Make sure you're keeping a friendly, professional tone while talking with creditors, as this will help you build a better rapport with them. They'll also be a lot more willing to help you if you're nice to them. This can be a frustrating process for sure, but it's important that you keep your cool.

Depending on what your specific circumstances are, you may be eligible for loan forgiveness. This can *also* be quite the process, but it's definitely worth looking into. You should also be willing to set up a repayment plan with your creditor — and this plan should ideally work for both of you. This will show that you're committed to paying off your debt and will help you avoid having to pay any additional fees or penalties as well.

THE PROS AND CONS OF CREDIT REPAIR COMPANIES

There truly is a company for everything, isn't there? Credit repair companies exist to help people improve their credit scores by working with creditors and credit bureaus to properly address any negative information showing up on their credit reports. If you don't know how to dispute inaccuracies or are nervous about negotiating with creditors, it might be a good idea to seek guidance from a credit repair company. As long as you're working with a reputable company, they should be able to help you come up with a plan to get your credit score up over time.

One of the main advantages of using the services of a credit repair company is that it's often quicker and easier than trying to negotiate with creditors and disputing credit report errors on your own. If you're working with a credit repair company, you can pretty much guarantee that you'll be working with an expert. They've spent years dealing with credit bureaus and creditors, so they know the ropes better than anyone. They should also be able to offer you valuable advice on how to improve your credit score and give you the push you need to stay on the right track financially.

However, working with a credit repair company doesn't come without its drawbacks. Most of these companies tend to charge high fees, and these fees can add up pretty quickly — especially if you happen to need ongoing help over an extended period of time. It's also important to keep in mind that credit repair does not happen instantaneously, so you'll need to wait a bit before you see any major results. Some credit repair companies can also be quite scammy, so you'll want to make sure you're able to differentiate between legitimate credit repair companies and fraudulent ones. Ultimately, whether or not you decide to work with a credit repair company is up to you. Just make sure to do your research beforehand, and be prepared to deal with some fees!

Common Red Flags to Look For if You Hire a Credit Repair Service

The number one red flag to be aware of, should you decide to hire a credit repair service, is if the company demands payment upfront. Reputable credit repair companies will never ask for money upfront, as they're required to actually help you out before receiving any payment. If the company does not provide you with a contract, that's also a red flag that should make you stop in your tracks. Without a contract, there's bound to be a lot of confusion or misunderstandings, which could cause major problems down the line.

Another thing you'll want to be wary of is companies that suggest taking illegal actions to repair your credit. This is obviously pretty sketchy, but you'd be surprised. Some fraudulent companies will get people to dispute accurate information on their credit reports or create new credit identities altogether. Please don't fall for this. The last thing you want to do is end up in jail when all you were trying to do was repair your credit score.

It's always a good idea to check and see if there have been any public complaints filed against the credit repair service you're considering hiring. You can easily check this with the Better Business Bureau or a similar protection agency. You should also, of course, be cautious of credit repair companies that promise something that seems too good to be true. Remember, scams *always* seem too good to be true. Credit repair is a process that takes time and effort. If you connect with a company that promises an easy fix overnight, chances are they're trying to scam you.

Credit Mastery Habit #5:

Action Step: Identify any errors or inaccuracies on your credit report and initiate disputes.

In order to establish this credit mastery habit, the first thing you should do is review your credit report and identify any discrepancies. If you find any errors, contact the credit bureau and request a dispute. This might take some time, but stick with it. It's well worth it to go through the entire process. When making your claim, you'll need to make sure to provide any and all necessary documentation to the credit bureau. Once your dispute has been resolved, continue to check your credit report to ensure that the errors have actually been removed. You should check your credit report at least once a month just to make sure everything is up-to-date and accurate. It should be pretty easy to get into the habit of doing so!

SEGUE

A lot of people suffer from poor credit scores because they simply don't understand what's contributing to their bad credit in the first place. It's all too common for people to neglect their bills, max out their credit cards, and apply for credit too often — and all of these things can cause one's credit score to take a dive. If you want to stay on top of your credit, you should also be checking your credit report for errors fairly regularly. You'll want to dispute any inaccuracies you come across sooner rather than later, as these inaccuracies can negatively affect your credit score. In the next chapter, I'll discuss some lesser-known credit-building hacks. Again, there's no overnight fix for bad credit, but these tips and tricks should help!

SKYROCKET YOUR SCORE WITH CREDIT BUILDING HACKS

Now, I'm not going to feed you the "build your credit lightning fast with this one simple trick!" kind of shtick because that's simply not how building credit works. Building credit is a marathon, not a sprint. It can take years to build up your credit score, especially if you're looking to join the 800 club — and that's okay! While it's true that older Americans have had more time to establish good credit, young people can also achieve high credit scores, especially if they're able to start building credit early.

Unfortunately, a lot of young Americans miss the opportunity to learn about proper credit management and how to build up credit in the first place. I've known way too many young people who've had to invest huge amounts of their time, money, and effort into fixing their credit — just so they could rent an apartment or get approved for loans. I want you to know that while things may seem bleak at the moment, turning your life around and getting your credit score up is entirely possible.

Take the story of Becky Beach, the owner of MomBeach.com, for example. When Becky was 18, she received a credit card in the mail, and despite the fact she didn't have a job yet, she began maxing it out and "going wild" without really thinking about the consequences. When her credit statement eventually arrived, she couldn't afford to make any payments, and her credit score suffered as a result.

Becky realized that she had messed up big time. She needed to take action right away if she was going to rebuild her credit score. After finding a job, she started paying the minimum amount on her monthly payments, which unfortunately ate up most of her paycheck — but she knew that she was simply reaping the consequences of her actions. After eight long years of making consistent payments, the blemish on her credit report disappeared. She was finally able to establish a good credit score and buy a house with her partner.

Becky's story serves as a good reminder that building credit takes a lot of time and patience. Due to her mistakes in the past, she had to live below her means and use most of her biweekly paycheck to pay off her credit card debt. She persevered, though, and eventually made peace with her past financial choices. She disputed the negative history on her credit report and sought help from a credit counselor so that she could consolidate her payments into more manageable chunks.

If you're in a situation similar to Becky's, don't give up hope. You have the power to change your financial situation for the better, and I'm about to give you the tools you need to do so. Once again, keep in mind that it isn't going to be an instant fix. That said, if you take these credit-building hacks into account while also being vigilant about staying on top of your credit card and loan payments, you should be well on your way to seeing your credit score climb to 800 and beyond. Let's get started, shall we?

THE POWER OF PIGGYBACKING ON SOMEONE ELSE'S GOOD CREDIT

In a sense, you're never too old to ask someone for a piggyback ride. Piggybacking is a commonly used credit-boosting technique that involves becoming an authorized user on someone else's credit card. This is not the same thing as having a joint account holder, though it's easy to see why people confuse the two. The main difference here is that an authorized user is not legally responsible for the charges that occur on the credit card, whereas a joint account holder would be responsible for those charges.

The idea behind piggybacking is that an authorized user can still benefit from having the account history reflected on their credit report despite not actually being responsible for any charges. This can be an excellent way to build your credit score, as long as the person your piggybacking off of has a healthy payment history and a good credit utilization rate. In general, you should only become an authorized user on someone else's account if you trust that person deeply. They should also, of course, have a positive credit history, or else piggybacking off of them could actually hurt your credit score.

When it comes to piggybacking on someone else's good credit, there are essentially two ways you can go about it: person-to-person piggybacking and for-profit piggybacking. I'll go over both in a bit more detail below so you can get a better idea of which piggybacking method will work best for you based on your specific situation.

Person-to-Person Piggybacking

If you haven't built up very much credit history, your mom, dad, or significant other (assuming they have good credit) would probably be happy to let you become an authorized user on their credit card. In order to make this happen, the person with good credit would need to contact their credit card issuer and add you as an authorized user. From there, you can choose whether or not you want to get your own card for the account. If you do decide to get a card, there will be certain privileges that come with it (depending on the credit card issuer). For example, an authorized user on a Citibank credit card will be able to make charges and payments on the account they're piggybacking off of — which is incredibly convenient.

If you're considering trying out person-to-person piggybacking, you're going to want to make sure that you're choosing the right person to piggyback off of. It may be safer to piggyback off of a parent or family friend than your significant other, especially if you haven't been in that particular relationship for a very long time. If you become an authorized user on their account and there's a rift in the relationship, or your partner falls on hard times, your credit score could end up suffering significantly.

For-Profit Piggybacking

Not everyone has the option of piggybacking off of their family or friends, and if this is the case for you, you can consider utilizing the services of a tradeline credit repair company. These companies charge a fee and match you with a cardholder who has an excellent credit score. The cardholder adds you to their credit card account as an authorized user and allows you to piggyback off of them in order to build your credit. The cardholder receives a portion of the fee you pay, and you won't receive an actual card — so it's definitely a bit different from person-to-person piggybacking.

Tradeline credit repair companies are... controversial to say the least. If you choose to go the for-profit piggybacking route, you'll be renting credit from a stranger who's essentially looking to make a profit from their great credit score. You'll also be using a for-profit business as an intermediary. I'm not saying for-profit piggybacking is a bad thing, but you're going to want to do thorough research on tradeline credit repair companies before making your choice. You've also, unfortunately, got to consider the fact that the stranger you're renting credit from may not have your best interests in mind.

HOW TO USE SECURED CREDIT CARDS TO BUILD CREDIT

If you're struggling to build your credit, you can always apply for a secured credit card. A lot of young people decide to get a secured credit card because it's a risk-free way to build credit. Unlike with unsecured credit cards, if you get a secured credit card, you'll be required to make a deposit upfront (which acts as collateral against the credit limit). Secured credit cards are actually quite similar to debit cards. The main difference is they can help you build your credit because the card issuer reports your payment history to the credit bureaus. Basically, every time you make a payment on time, your credit score goes up. Of course, if you miss a payment, your credit score is likely to take a hit.

One of the main benefits of using a secured credit card is that it doesn't pose any risk to you. You're required to make that upfront deposit, so the card issuer has already been reimbursed for any charges you end up making. This also means that if you fail to make a payment, your card issuer can simply subtract the amount from your deposit. You also don't need to have good credit to get approved for a secured credit card. Again, this is because you're providing collateral. This means that secured credit cards are an especially accessible option for those who are only just starting to build their credit.

With a secured credit card, you'll also be able to get perks like travel and cash back rewards — just like you would with a regular credit card. Not only that, but using a secured credit card can be a great way to help you build responsible credit payment habits, and this will give lenders confidence that you'll be ready to handle an unsecured credit card in the future. Just remember to make on-time payments and keep your credit utilization low. There's still a lot of responsibility that comes with using a secured credit card!

Best Practices for Using Secured Credit Cards to Build Credit

I would absolutely recommend using a secured credit card to help build your credit, but it's super important that you know how to use this type of credit card correctly. Let's go over some tips that will help you make the most out of using your secured credit card (while also staying out of trouble) below:

Pick the Right Secured Card

Ah, yes. This brings us back to the importance of reading the terms and conditions carefully before you apply for a credit card. Despite the fact that secured credit cards don't come with much of a risk factor, there are some secured cards that have higher fees and rates than traditional credit cards do. Take some time to read all of the terms and conditions before you apply for a specific secured card. I know this isn't the most exhilarating activity in the world, but trust me. It's worth it!

Pay the Deposit Quickly

It may be a good idea to start saving up so you can make your collateral deposit in full. This will allow you to establish your credit limit and start using your secured credit card right away. Also, if you make this deposit quickly, it'll show lenders that you're responsible with money and are able to make on-time payments without an issue.

Watch Your Spending

Although you'll be paying a deposit upfront when you apply for a secured credit card, you're still going to want to keep track of your spending. It's generally a good idea to keep your balance at 30% or less of your credit limit. This will show lenders that you're responsible with credit and help you avoid falling into a pit of debt.

Always Pay in Full

While a secured credit card is slightly different from a traditional credit card, they still tend to come with interest charges. Thankfully, you can avoid these interest charges by paying your balance in full every month. If you're late on any payments (or miss a payment altogether), this can damage your credit score. As with a regular credit card, staying on top of your secured credit card payments is key!

Stay Consistent

As I've already mentioned (probably too many times at this point), building credit takes time. It also requires you to be consistent with your spending habits and monthly payments. Make sure you're using your secured credit card regularly, and again, make your payments on time every month. In time, you should start to see your credit score go up.

THE IMPACT OF CREDIT LIMITS ON YOUR CREDIT SCORE

If you've ever used a credit card, you're probably well aware that you have a credit limit. In case you don't know, a credit limit refers to the maximum amount of money you're allowed to borrow or spend using your credit card or another line of credit. Your credit limit can affect your credit score in significant ways, and your financial future depends largely on how you decide to use your credit card. Although you probably know your credit limit, it's not a good idea to max out your credit card, as this can have a negative impact on your credit score. If you can learn how to properly and responsibly manage your credit limit *now*, however, you should be able to improve your chances of getting approved for things like car loans and mortgages in the future.

A lot of people have come to find that not maxing out their credit card is more difficult than they ever imagined it would be. Emergencies happen, and life moves fast. You'd be surprised how quickly the limit on your credit card can run out, especially if you don't keep track of your spending. One thing you can do to keep your credit utilization low and avoid maxing out your credit card(s) is to increase your credit limit(s). Let's take a closer look at why you might want to do this below:

Helps With Emergencies

Naturally, having a credit limit that's higher than what you usually spend can be super helpful in emergency situations. Imagine you're on a trip abroad, and you suddenly need to buy a new plane ticket and come back home as soon as possible because of a medical emergency. Or, what if you get in a car accident, and your car ends up needing an expensive repair that you didn't budget for? In these types of cases, having a credit card with a higher limit can truly be a lifesaver. You should set up an emergency fund in case they do find themselves in these types of situations, but you may be in the process of building one. If you have a higher credit limit, you'll be able to cover emergency costs while also maintaining a relatively low credit utilization rate.

You Can Earn More Rewards

If you're the type of person who pays their credit card balance in full and on time every month, but you're not putting *all* of your expenses on your card, you may want to consider doing so. This could be a great way to increase the rewards you earn (like cash back), so it's definitely worth it. Some people might tell you not to use your credit card for everyday expenses like gas and groceries, but this is really only an issue if you're carrying a balance. If you're not carrying a balance, there's no harm in using your card for these types of things, and it can actually help you earn more rewards in the long run. ***Be careful when doing this — your expenses can get out of hand very quickly. Start small and work your way up responsibly.***

You Won't Have to Worry When Making Large Purchases

You might already know that using your credit card to buy especially expensive things is fairly easy and can help you earn some pretty great rewards. Most people don't realize, however, that a lot of credit cards offer certain protections that can save you a lot of trouble if you run into any issues while making large purchases. For example, Mastercard offers extended warranties, price protection, and coverage in case what you purchased gets stolen. Essentially, having a higher credit limit can provide you with significant peace of mind when it comes to making those big (but necessary) purchases.

Avoid Credit Score Dings

Finally, increasing your credit limit is a fantastic way to avoid credit score dings. Of course, if you're looking to increase your credit, you could always just apply for another credit card — but as we've learned, this isn't necessarily the best option. While applying for a new credit card could lower your credit score, requesting an increase to your existing credit limit won't affect your score all that much. Opening a new credit card account shortens your credit history, which won't look very good to lenders. I'd definitely opt for increasing your existing credit if I were you!

THE IMPORTANCE OF DIVERSITY IN CREDIT ACCOUNTS

While relying solely on one type of credit account to build your credit history might sound ideal (for simplicity's sake), this is not actually a good idea. If you diversify your credit accounts (i.e. have a mix of different types of credit in your name), you'll be able to build a stronger credit history and eventually increase your credit score. If you have different types of accounts to keep track of — and you're able to manage all of your different payments responsibly — this will show lenders that you're capable of juggling lots of different types of debt.

As I mentioned before, there are a few different types of credit that count toward your credit score, namely revolving debt and mortgage loans. It's a good idea to include revolving debt (i.e. credit cards) in your mix of different credit accounts, as paying off your credit card account (potentially with interest) every month shows immense responsibility. Similarly, taking out a mortgage loan and paying it back in full over a period of time will show lenders that you're able to handle large, long-term debts.

Open accounts — like your phone bill or monthly rent — don't count toward your credit score by default. However, if these accounts are sent to a collection agency, they may be included in your credit report. Again, including open accounts in your credit report can help to diversify your credit history and demonstrate to lenders that you've mastered the art of juggling multiple different types of credit.

A NOTE ON CREDIT INQUIRIES

I've briefly gone over credit inquiries already, but I find it necessary to stress the various reasons why they matter so much. To reiterate, a credit inquiry is a review of your credit report (typically by lenders and landlords), which includes your credit history and lets those making an inquiry know whether or not you're responsible for using credit and making on-time payments. Essentially, when you apply for a loan, credit card, or new apartment, the companies involved want to know that you're reliable (i.e. *not* a financial risk).

There are two types of credit inquiries: hard inquiries and soft inquiries. Hard inquiries can make your credit score go down temporarily and tend to occur when you apply for a loan or new credit card. Soft inquiries, on the other hand, don't affect your credit score at all. These types of inquiries mainly occur when someone runs a background check on you or when you make a personal inquiry into your own credit history.

Credit Mastery Habit #6:

Action Step: Implement at least two credit-building hacks into your financial routine.

In order to implement a couple of the aforementioned credit-building hacks into your financial routine, you're going to want to start by deciding which hacks will best suit your personal situation. I'd recommend either becoming an authorized user on your friend's or family member's credit card or using a secured credit card to build credit in a risk-free way. You can also choose to increase your credit limit on one of your existing cards or diversify your credit mix by taking out a small loan or opening up a new credit card account. Make sure to keep track of your credit utilization rate and pay off your balances in full every month. Once you've picked out some strategies that will work best for you, try to make them a part of your daily or weekly routine. In time, you'll see that these habits will become second nature to you!

SEGUE

If you know how to go about it, getting your credit score up isn't so difficult after all. I'd recommend picking and choosing the hacks that stand out to you in particular and implementing them into your routine in a way that's manageable. Go with your gut, and don't try to utilize more credit-building hacks than you can handle at one time. Remember: slow and steady wins the race. In the next chapter, I'll talk about what you can do to maintain good credit once you've gotten your credit score up.

7

MAINTAINING YOUR SOARING CREDIT SCORE

When it comes to maintaining a fantastic credit score, you're going to want to take the advice that Gandalf the Grey gave Frodo regarding the one ring to rule them all: "Keep it secret. Keep it safe." Okay, so you don't actually need to keep your credit score a secret, but keeping it safe is essential. It's not as if everyone in Middle Earth is trying to get their hands on your credit score, but you'd be surprised how fragile a great credit score can be. There are a lot of common mistakes people end up making — mistakes that, to their surprise, lower their scores — so you're definitely going to want to be aware of these mistakes and avoid them at all costs.

Allow me to share a story with you that really got me thinking about the importance of protecting my credit score. This is something that happened to my good friend, Blake, and he's given me permission to share it here. I'll start out by saying that Blake had always been super responsible — with his work, his personal life, and his finances. He worked hard to save up for a down payment on his dream home and, after years of searching, eventually found exactly what he was looking for. The only problem was his credit score was just shy of the minimum score required to secure a mortgage.

Blake was determined not to let this setback ruin his plans, though, so he began researching ways that he could improve his credit score. He eventually stumbled upon an article that suggested paying off his student loans might boost his credit score. He thought to himself: *Okay, great — I can do that!* And, without further ado, he paid off the remainder of his student loans. At first, everything seemed to be going according to plan for Blake. He watched his credit score slowly increase and felt confident about his decision to pay off his student loans.

Just as he was getting ready to close on his dream home, however, his credit score suddenly plummeted. In what felt like the blink of an eye, Blake was no longer eligible for the mortgage he had worked so hard to secure. He immediately contacted his lender to try to figure out what had happened. It turned out that paying off his student loans had actually hurt his credit score because his student loans were the only type of installment debt he had on his credit record. By paying it off, he had inadvertently lowered his credit mix, which lowered his credit score by about 30 or 40 points.

Needless to say, Blake was desperate to salvage the situation. He wracked his brain trying to think of ways to *actually* boost his credit score. He tried asking his credit card company for a limit increase and paid off all of his credit card debt, but no matter what he did, his score wouldn't budge. He eventually had to accept the fact that his dream home was out of reach — at least for the time being. He had to put that particular dream on hold and focus on rebuilding his credit score from scratch. "This was a grueling process," he told me. "But I got there, eventually."

Today, Blake is living in a beautiful home with his wife and two children (with another on the way). This entire experience made him realize that sometimes, even the most responsible financial decisions can have unintended consequences. From then on, he made sure to always consult with financial experts before making any major financial decisions, as he certainly didn't want to find himself in that same situation again. He checks his credit score pretty religiously and is vigilant about paying all of his bills and credit card payments on time. "Your credit score can change like *that*," he said, snapping his fingers. "You've got to stay on top of it because you just never know what could happen."

In this section, I'll be going over the importance of monitoring your credit score. I'll also be delving into how to protect yourself from identity theft, which is a huge issue, and could give you quite the scare if you're not properly prepared to deal with it. By the end of this chapter, you'll know how to establish a monthly routine for monitoring your credit score. I'll also give you the space — the "permission" or *sign* you've been waiting for, so to speak — to set up alerts for your credit score changes. Let's get started.

THE IMPORTANCE OF CONTINUING TO MONITOR YOUR CREDIT SCORE

Even if you're not in a good place financially right now, monitoring your credit score closely and regularly is incredibly important. Think about it this way: if you monitor your credit score, you'll be able to catch any incorrect information or mistakes on your credit report before they become a real problem. Credit reports are oftentimes not perfect. Errors happen, and these errors can lower your credit score and sometimes lead to things like loan denials and higher interest rates. Let's take a closer look at the main benefits of continuing to monitor your credit score below:

You'll Be Aware of What Lenders See When They Review Your Credit Report

As you already know by this point, your credit score is a direct reflection of your creditworthiness. Lenders use your credit score to determine whether or not you'll be trustworthy when it comes to paying back loans or credit card debt. Naturally, you'll want to make sure that the information on your credit report is accurate and up-to-date. You don't want lenders to get the wrong idea just because someone made a mistake on your credit report. This is one of the main reasons why regular monitoring is so important!

You Can Check For Fraud

By monitoring your credit score regularly, you'll also be ensuring that you haven't fallen victim to fraud or identity theft. Identity theft and credit card fraud are unfortunately super common occurrences, and if left unchecked, these issues — no, *crimes* — can wreak serious havoc on your credit score. Thankfully, if you're willing to take the time to monitor your credit score and review your credit report regularly, you should be able to put a quick stop to any suspicious activity that you happen to come across.

It Will Improve Your Financial Health Overall

Being in control of your financial health feels good. Right now, you might feel like you have very little control over your finances. I've been there, too, but trust me — keeping a close eye on your credit score is a great way to track your progress and figure out what's actually working in terms of the strategies you've been using to try and increase your score. As you watch your score tick up, you'll likely feel a lot more motivated and focused on your financial goals, and, in time, you should be able to achieve financial comfort. I'm not saying this will be easy, but it *will* be worth it. You know it will.

HOW TO PROTECT YOUR CREDIT SCORE FROM IDENTITY THEFT

If you're afraid of being a victim of identity theft, just know you're not alone and that that fear is totally valid. Identity theft is scary! Oftentimes, it can hit you out of nowhere, and if you don't protect your credit score and monitor your credit report regularly, your score could end up taking a serious hit. Not many people know this, but there are actually a lot of different types of identity theft out there. Let's take a look at these different types so that you can better understand them and protect yourself more effectively:

Child Identity Theft

This is when someone uses a child's Social Security number to commit fraud. This type of identity theft can go unnoticed for years because children, of course, don't generally have credit reports. If you want to protect your kid from identity theft, you should check whether or not they actually *do* have a credit report, as this could be an indication that their identity has been stolen.

Synthetic Identity Theft

Synthetic identity theft is a very sneaky form of fraud in which the thief will use a real person's Social Security number and then make up a name, date of birth, email address, and mailing address to create a new identity. Like child identity theft, this type of identity theft can be difficult to detect. The victims of synthetic identity theft tend to be older folks and houseless people, as they may not have the ability to properly monitor their credit reports.

Credit Identity Theft

This type of identity theft is pretty common. If you've ever noticed any unauthorized purchases on your credit card, you've likely been a victim of credit identity theft. Needless to say, it's very important that you keep your credit card information safe. Don't share it with any random people or sketchy websites! If you do happen to do so, you'll want to call your bank immediately — especially if you notice any charges on your card that you didn't make.

Medical Identity Theft

As the name suggests, this type of identity theft is when someone uses your medical information to receive medical treatment. This is obviously pretty serious, as it can cause problems with your medical care as well as waste a lot of money. Remember to keep information like your Medicare number and Social Security number private since that's all the information an identity thief will need to steal your medical identity.

Account Takeover

This is when someone gains access to your existing accounts and starts making a bunch of unauthorized changes. This basically makes it possible for the thief to then steal your bank or credit card information. If you suddenly get bombarded with phishing emails or start to notice multiple log-in attempts on your account(s), you'll want to be especially wary of this type of identity theft.

STEPS TO PROTECT YOURSELF

Technology is getting more and more advanced, so it's no surprise that cybercrime is on the rise. You might feel like setting long, complicated passwords with a lot of different numbers and characters for all of your accounts is overkill — but it's really not. Hackers are getting better and better at what they do, so it's only natural that we should kick it up a notch or two when it comes to protecting ourselves. Let's take a look at some steps you can take to better protect yourself from identity theft below:

Contact Companies Immediately

If you believe that your credit card account has been compromised, you should call your bank or credit card company as soon as possible. They're trained to handle situations like this, so they should be able to help you protect your accounts and prevent further damage — as long as you're able to fill them in on as much as you know about the situation.

Check Your Credit Report Regularly

I've been drilling this point into your head for a reason. Regularly checking your credit report is *really, really* important. If you make a point of checking your credit report religiously, you'll have a much easier time catching any issues or unauthorized changes before things begin to spiral out of control. You may also want to set up a fraud alert so that the credit bureaus notify you before opening any new accounts in your name.

Freeze Your Accounts if Necessary

If a lot of damage has already been done, you might want to consider freezing your accounts until you figure out what your next action step will be. This can, unfortunately, be a pretty time-consuming process, but it's definitely worth it to protect your finances. You should also file a police report, as that will help to prevent similar incidents from taking place in the future.

Use Biometric Payment Methods

Using biometric payment methods is an absolute must if you're going to be truly vigilant about protecting yourself from identity theft. This technology (i.e. fingerprint or facial recognition) tends to make it a lot of difficult for fraudsters to steal your information. It's also more convenient than having to type in a password every single time you need to access your account(s).

Remove Unnecessary Identification From Your Wallet

Although you may be tempted to carry around your social security card in your wallet "for safekeeping," this is actually not the best idea. It's obviously devastating when your wallet gets stolen — regardless of what you have in there — but by taking out any identification that you don't actually need to carry around with you all the time (i.e. old credit cards, insurance cards, etc.) you'll be able to more efficiently protect yourself against identity theft.

Be Especially Careful Online

Phishing attempts and scams are more prevalent now than ever before, and they can honestly be pretty difficult to spot if you don't know what to look for. You should always be wary of any emails or texts that tell you to click on sketchy links (or right out ask for your personal information). Remember to double-check any requests for sensitive information and block numbers that text you at 3 AM asking you to click on a weird link.

WHAT HAPPENS WHEN YOU CLOSE A CREDIT ACCOUNT?

Ah, yes. The age-old question. What happens when you close a credit account? Not everyone knows this, but closing your credit account can lower your overall credit limit, which in turn, can increase your credit utilization rate. This is likely to have a short-term negative impact on your credit score since your credit utilization rate is one of the main factors used to calculate your credit score in the first place. Closing an account can also, unfortunately, affect the length of your credit history since accounts that you've closed will usually get removed from your credit report after a set amount of time.

You'll also want to take your credit mix into account if you're thinking about closing a credit account. Naturally, closing a credit account can end up making your credit mix appear rather limited, which isn't great for your credit score as a whole. "I have to close this particular account, though," you might be thinking right now. "What, you're saying I can't?" No, dear reader, that's not what I'm saying. It's just that you should have a good reason for closing a credit account (i.e. divorce, high fees, or too much temptation). You should also pay off all of the remaining balances across all of your cards so that you can minimize your utilization rate when you finally cancel the account that's causing you trouble.

Before canceling your account, you'll want to call your credit card company and make sure that your balance is actually at $0. You may also want to have a certified letter mailed to you confirming the $0 balance just to cover all of your bases.

Credit Mastery Habit #7:

Action Step: Establish a monthly credit monitoring routine and set up alerts for credit score changes.

Establishing a monthly credit monitoring routine is super important as far as maintaining healthy credit goes. The first thing you'll need to do is set up alerts for any changes that take place in your credit score. This will be a great way to ensure that you're notified immediately of any changes, which means you'll be able to take action quickly if something happens. You should also, of course, monitor your credit report regularly, keep your credit utilization rate low by making on-time payments, and avoid any unnecessary credit applications. By establishing a regular credit monitoring routine and setting up some much-needed alerts, you'll be able to take control of your credit and maintain a healthy credit score.

SEGUE

Inaccuracies or unauthorized changes that come up on your credit report can be panic-inducing since these issues are oftentimes an indication that you're under threat of identity theft. Thankfully, there are plenty of ways to protect yourself from identity theft, especially these days. Remember to check your credit report regularly, and follow the aforementioned steps to keep yourself safe! In the next chapter, I'll be going over some of the most common myths and misconceptions surrounding credit scores.

8

THE TRUTH ABOUT CREDIT SCORES: MYTHS, MISCONCEPTIONS, AND MISTAKES

When I was 20, I moved out of my mom's house and applied for a bunch of different apartments. Every single landlord asked me, "How's your credit?" to which I had no choice but respond with: "Uh… I don't really have credit." Obviously, this made it really difficult to find an apartment. My guess is that this is a pretty typical experience for people in their late teens and early 20s. As per the data revealed by the Consumer Financial Protection Bureau (CFPB), around 26 million Americans don't have any credit history and are often referred to as "credit invisible" for this reason.

This means that they've never had any information reported to the three major credit bureaus, which, needless to say, can pose difficulties if they need to access a line of credit or — in my 20-year-old case —

apply for an apartment. Now, being "credit invisible" doesn't necessarily imply that you have a credit score of zero. What this really means is that you don't have a credit score at all. Yes, there's a difference!

If you don't have any credit history, that does not necessarily indicate that you're financially irresponsible or that you've never paid any bills. It simply means that none of the bills you've paid have been reported to the three credit bureaus. There are a lot of reasons why a young person, in particular, might not have any credit history. Perhaps you prefer to pay for everything in cash, or you've never had a credit card. A lack of credit history isn't necessarily a negative reflection on you, but it will, ultimately, make your life harder in the long run.

Even when you do eventually obtain a line of credit, it's going to take some time for your credit score to appear on your credit report. In fact, it can take as long as six months for a FICO score (which is used by 90% of lenders) to show up on your report. This is why having no credit history can create a prolonged problem, even after you've opened up your first credit account. This is all in the realm of the lack of understanding surrounding credit scores and the mistakes people tend to make because of the misconceptions they've developed. In this section, I'll go over some of the myths you'll likely come across while attempting to build up your credit score. The more aware you are of these myths, the more you'll be able to avoid falling victim to bad credit habits!

THE MYTHS SURROUNDING CREDIT SCORES

I feel like one of the main reasons why credit and credit scores create so much confusion among the general public is that there are so many myths and misconceptions out there that lead people to unintentionally harm their own financial standing. Some believe that you have to carry a balance to build credit, and others think that only rich people have good credit scores — neither of which is true. I don't want you to have to agonize over separating fact from fiction, so let's take a minute to debunk some of the most common credit score myths you're likely to come across below.

Myth #1: You Should Carry a Balance to Build Credit

Carrying a balance on your credit card is actually not an effective way to improve your credit score. In fact, it may end up doing more harm than good. If you accrue interest on your debt, you could actually end up with a higher debt utilization rate, which (as you know by now) is a key factor in determining credit scores.

Younger generations are far more likely to believe in this misconception. According to Credit Beliefs Survey, 38.7% of Gen X, 48.3% of Millennials, and a staggering 52.5% of Gen Z respondents believe that carrying a balance will help build their credit. Making mistakes with credit at a young age can have serious consequences, so make sure that you keep paying off your card balances in full!

Myth #2: Checking Your Credit Negatively Affects Your Score

Some people believe that checking your credit score can actually lower it since checking your score is considered to be an "inquiry." The truth is that checking your own credit score is considered a "soft inquiry" and does not actually harm your score — so feel free to check your score as often as you'd like to. That said, too many "hard inquiries," like those made by lenders when you apply for new lines of credit, *can* negatively affect your score.

Myth #3: How Much You Make Influences Your Score

Contrary to popular belief, your income and job title don't have any sort of direct impact on your credit score. As previously mentioned, your score is based solely on the data in your credit report, which lets lenders know how you handle credit and debt payments. It doesn't factor in your income, and, more than likely, it won't even indicate your employment status.

Myth #4: Only Rich People Have Good Credit Scores

On a similar note, people tend to assume that only wealthy people have good credit scores. This is not true at all. In fact, a lot of rich people have bad credit scores because of their irresponsible spending habits. Anyone can have a good credit score as long as they're being responsible with their spending and paying their bills on time, regardless of how much money they happen to have.

Myth #5: Paying Off Debt Automatically Increases Your Credit Score

Having a lot of debt is obviously stressful, and while paying off your debt is important for your financial health as a whole, doing so probably won't automatically increase your credit score. It may — but it really depends on your credit history. Sometimes, paying off your debt can be a good way to improve your credit utilization rate, which could slightly increase your credit score. Remember, this process is slow and steady. Keep paying off your debts while *also* making your credit card payments on time, and you should see your credit score go up.

Myth #6: Closing Credit Card Accounts Can Help Boost Your Score

Once again, closing your credit card accounts will not increase your credit score! I really can't stress this one enough. Closing your credit card accounts can actually hurt your credit score, especially if the account you're closing has a long credit history. Sometimes, you can't really avoid closing a certain account, but if you can, you should try to keep your accounts open and use your credit responsibly. This will help to improve your credit utilization rate (and your credit score).

Credit Mastery Habit #8:

Action Step: Identify one myth or mistake that's led to a decision you regret.

If you've made a financial decision related to credit in the last 30 days that you now regret, I'd strongly recommend taking some time to reflect on what led you to make that decision. Consider what you could have done differently and what you *will* do differently when a similar situation comes up. Once you've figured out what your specific issues are with maintaining a good credit score, commit to establishing some habits that will help you make better decisions in the future. These habits could include creating a monthly budget, setting up automatic payments, or simply taking a pause before making a certain purchase. Make a plan for what you will do differently over the next month, and avoid mistakes similar to the ones you made previously.

SEGUE

Now that you're aware of the main myths that people find themselves getting caught up in whilst navigating the complex world of credit scores, you shouldn't have any trouble staying on track when it comes to increasing your score and bettering your financial health. Take some time to reflect on your past mistakes and make a solid plan for the next month regarding your budget, your credit card payments, and your spending habits. The next chapter should help you out with this, as I'll be delving into some habits that people with credit scores of 800 and beyond tend to live by.

9

BONUS — HABITS OF THE 800 CLUB: SECRETS OF THE CREDIT ELITE

Leslie Tayne, an accomplished attorney, was saddled with crippling student loan debt and a husband who insisted on controlling their shared finances. Everything was under his name, even the car she drove, and despite the fact that he was the one who wanted to be in charge of their finances, he wasn't paying off Tayne's law school debt. She was eventually sued by her lender because of this, which, as you can imagine, got her into even deeper trouble.

After getting divorced from her husband, she was determined to pay off her debt and get her credit score up. She struggled to make her monthly payments, which was especially tough because she'd just started a family. A lot of her money was going to babysitting and feeding her kids, but she persevered and was slowly but surely able to get her credit score over 800 — a feat that only about 21% of credit holders in the United States have managed to accomplish.

Today, Tayne owns her own debt resolution firm and helps people who are in similar situations to her own improve their finances. She continuously preaches the value of taking baby steps and taking an individualized approach when it comes to fixing one's damaged credit score. I'm sharing her story here because it's a testament to the fact that hard work pays off. No matter what your situation is, overcoming your financial struggles and obtaining the credit score you've always wanted is possible. You may have to grit your teeth and live below your means for a while, but it will ultimately be worth it.

WHO ARE THE MEMBERS OF THE 800 CLUB?

As the name suggests, the "800 Club" refers to those who have a credit score of 800 or higher. Around 20% of Americans belong to the 800 Club. It's generally quite difficult to get to this point, and a lot of people in this group will tell you that they basically worked tooth and nail to get their score above 800. As you may have already guessed, those who are in the 800 Club tend to have exceptional financial responsibility, usually over a long period of time. If you're able to get your credit score this high, you'll be able to qualify for the best credit cards and secure the lowest interest rates on loans — so it's definitely worth it.

Contrary to popular belief, the 800 Club doesn't just include people who are rich or who have never taken out any loans in their life. Anyone can join the 800 Club, so no matter what you're circumstances are, it's absolutely something to strive for. You're well aware of this by this point, but building and maintaining a fantastic credit score requires exceptional discipline and patience. It's not something that's going to happen overnight, but it's doable for *anyone*. Try to keep that in mind as you work towards your financial goals.

Naturally, if you're going to join the 800 Club, you're going to want to start making on-time payments and diversifying your credit accounts as much as you can. You should also, of course, keep your credit utilization low and minimize your credit inquiries. Chances are, your credit score will fluctuate here and there based on where your life takes you, but in time — and if you're able to develop the right habits — you'll find yourself joining the ranks of this elite group.

THE HABITS AND PRACTICES OF THOSE WITH EXCELLENT CREDIT SCORES

Studies have consistently shown that people with higher-than-average credit scores receive the best interest rates, excellent loan terms, and fantastic opportunities compared to those who have average or below-average scores. As I mentioned before, building your credit score up to 800 and beyond is no easy task, but it's attainable if you're willing to change up your lifestyle and spending habits a bit. Let's take a closer look at some of the habits those with excellent credit scores have implemented into their lives below:

Credit Monitoring Plan

People in the 800 Club are notoriously fantastic about keeping a close eye on their credit scores and staying on top of their payments and credit monitoring plans. You may not have a credit monitoring plan in place right now, but coming up with one should be fairly straightforward. A credit monitoring plan can provide you with regular updates and alerts, so you'll never be caught off guard by changes or inquiries that show up on your credit report. By implementing a credit monitoring plan, you'll be able to remain vigilant when it comes to maintaining the health of your credit. Talk to your bank about setting up a credit monitoring plan when you get the chance. They'll be happy to help!

Disciplined With Finances in General

People with high credit scores also tend to be very disciplined with how they manage their finances. This shouldn't come as too much of a surprise. Those in the 800 Club are oftentimes quite proactive when it comes to setting realistic financial goals. It's also worth mentioning that they're truly committed to achieving these goals. They understand that making sacrifices is a necessity and are generally less prone to impulsive spending than those with lower credit scores. People with average or below-average credit scores might view credit as "extra" money, whereas those in the 800 Club will tend to have the opposite mindset. If you want to work towards adopting this mindset, you're going to need to shift your priorities. People with high credit scores typically prioritize their long-term financial goals (i.e. homeownership or saving for retirement) over their short-term goals.

Start Early

Starting early is key when it comes to building and maintaining an excellent credit score. According to

Heather Battison, the Vice President at TransUnion, obtaining a stellar credit score requires both patience and unwavering financial discipline. She emphasizes the importance of establishing a personal financial management process that incorporates credit management as a fundamental aspect. People who get to boast high credit scores often embarked on their financial journey fairly early on and adopted practices like creating a budget, being mindful of their spending, and consistently making on-time credit card payments. I would highly suggest opening a credit card account while you're still young, but you *must* be diligent about paying off your balance in full each month. This will slowly help you build up your credit history.

Use a Budget For Everything

If you want to eventually achieve an outstanding credit score, you're going to need to embrace a lifestyle that aligns with your financial means. This will involve creating a weekly or monthly budget for yourself so that you can easily track your inflow of money and make good decisions regarding your spending and saving. When creating a budget, make sure to prioritize things like bills, rent, food, and other necessary expenses. Put aside some money for savings every time you get your paycheck, and think twice before making purchases that seem frivolous.

Cross-Check Credit Scores

A big part of obtaining an excellent credit score is, of course, familiarizing yourself with your current credit score. Plenty of financial institutions, like Capital One, for example, will provide you with free access to credit score tracking tools — so you'll never be in the dark about where you're at in terms of your creditworthiness. You can also request a free credit report from any of the three major credit bureaus, either online or via snail mail. Thoroughly review your credit reports once you receive them, as you'll want to make sure that they don't contain any incorrect information. Errors happen, and while they're relatively easy to fix, it's always best to nip them in the bud as soon as possible.

Consolidate Debt

If you have a significant amount of debt, you may be able to improve your credit score (and just generally make things easier on yourself) by consolidating it. Debt consolidation basically involves merging your debts from different lenders into one single debt, which typically comes with a lower interest rate. It may feel like this is a weighty decision — and it is — but it should also give you some clarity in terms of your debt payments and other financial obligations. I'd definitely recommend meeting with a credit counselor or working with a debt consolidation program if you're interested in going this route!

HOW TO ADOPT THE MINDSET OF THE CREDIT ELITE

Building up your credit score requires more than just the practical aspects (though these aspects are important for sure). It's also largely about adopting the right mindset. While positive thinking alone won't make your score go up (wouldn't that be nice), it will help you stay motivated and resilient while living by your new credit-building habits. Of course, adopting the mindset of the credit elite is easier said than done.

Effectively managing your money is a juggling act, and amidst this whirlwind, building credit can honestly feel like an additional burden. It will oftentimes be overshadowed by your other, "more pressing" financial obligations and this may cause you to feel like building your credit is just another time-consuming chore that you'd like to put off for another time. It's completely normal to feel this way. It's exactly how I felt throughout my twenties, and it took quite a bit of time to realize and acknowledge that this mindset wasn't healthy. Let's take a look at some strategies you can use to alter your mindset about building credit below:

Be Realistic With Yourself

Whether you're starting from scratch or rebuilding your credit score after going through identity theft or another financial calamity, it's essential that you understand that this process takes time. Patience is definitely a virtue, and you'll see this clear as day as you navigate through the choices you'll need to make in order to build up a healthier credit score. As I mentioned before, building credit or improving a damaged credit history requires exceptional dedication and perseverance. You'll need to acknowledge that visible results may not manifest immediately. In fact, it can take several months of consistent effort and responsible financial behavior before you see the fruits of your labor reflected in your credit score. If you accept this reality and adopt a more patient and realistic mindset, you'll be able to stay positive throughout this process — which will make things a whole lot easier!

Focus on Small Changes

Remember, you don't have to make a million lifestyle changes all at once. You're asking a lot of yourself, so it's best to wade into the water at your own pace, one toe at a time. If you usually buy lunch during work, try to get yourself into the routine of preparing meals beforehand at home. Make gradual changes to your usual grocery list, and restrain yourself when it comes to impulse buys. Each week, aim to introduce one of two small changes into your spending routine that you're absolutely sure you'll be able to follow through on. You'll eventually get used to your new spending habits and lifestyle, and this will help you maintain the mindset you need to obtain an excellent credit score.

Work Towards Your Goals

It can be challenging to keep a positive financial mindset, especially if you happen to find yourself in an overwhelming — and expensive — situation. It's incredibly important, however, that you shift your perspective and focus on your goals while building up your credit. If your goal is to save money, for example, you should try to define a specific savings timeline and figure out the amount that you'll be able to realistically set aside each month. Calculate the time it will take you to reach your ultimate goal, and, most importantly, keep your eyes on the prize.

Think of Money Like a Plant

Although it may feel odd to think about it this way, money is quite like a plant. You shouldn't abuse it, and if you want it to grow, you need to put time and effort into nurturing it. Just like a garden, your financial health requires regular nourishment and maintenance to survive and thrive. While you need not obsess over every small financial detail, you should try to make informed and prudent decisions that will foster growth and stability as far as building up your savings account and credit score goes.

Focus on the Positive Outcomes of Building Credit in the Long Run

As I said before — keep your eyes on the prize, even if that prize is a long way off. Remember, you're not changing up your spending habits and altering your mindset towards building credit to torture yourself. You're doing this because it's an investment for your future. By building and maintaining an excellent credit score, you'll have access to better credit card and loan deals, and you'll likely have an easier time saving up for retirement or your future home as well. It will take time, of course, but stick with it. You'll get there.

THE IMPORTANCE OF DISCIPLINE AND CONSISTENCY

When you go to the gym to work out, surely you don't expect instant results. No one walks into the gym with the physique of Gumby and comes out looking like the Incredible Hulk in one single day. It takes a lot of time and effort to build up your physical muscles, and the same is true for your behavioral muscles. To use another analogy, building new habits is sort of like attempting to part your hair differently. It's going to be a little uncomfortable at first, but as time goes on, you'll fall into your new routine with ease. The thing about discipline is you begrudge it — that will only make you miserable and more prone to going against your new habits. You should instead embrace discipline, as that will help you build a lasting foundation for the healthy change you need in your life.

Basically, your discipline will protect you from yourself in the long run. It'll prevent you from stealing from your future self, which your future self will certainly thank you for. By exercising financial self-control, you'll be able to keep yourself from indulging in unnecessary expenses or falling into a pit of debt. Those who have managed to get into the exclusive 800 Club tend to prioritize saving, investing, and, overall, building a strong financial foundation — and you can too. Once again, this is easier said than done, but if you're able to apply discipline to the three pillars of wealth, that would be a very good place to start.

The first pillar of wealth involves managing your costs and spending wisely, which, as you may have guessed, will entail careful and constant evaluation of your expenses and making conscious decisions to live within (or even below) your means. The second pillar of wealth is all about investing *without* being swayed by your emotions, as this will ensure that your investment decisions are based on solid research and a good long-term perspective. Finally, the third pillar of wealth involves using your skills to increase your income as well as create additional sources of income for yourself. As you can see, being disciplined with your finances requires a lot of strategy. My hope is that by breaking down the three pillars of wealth for you, I've made this strategic approach a little easier to digest and implement into your lifestyle.

Keep in mind the role that compound interest plays in credit-building, and remember to make consistent and on-time payments on all of your debts and loans. Temptation is going to strike at some point, but try to restrain yourself from giving into impulsive spending. Indulging in your impulses will feel good in the moment, but you'll ultimately be jeopardizing your future and the growth of your credit score by doing so. Building up your discipline and implementing healthier financial habits into your lifestyle is not about forcing yourself into a rigid routine. It's about adopting one small habit at a time and stacking these habits as you get used to living by them. Every positive financial decision you make will build upon the last, so keep building! I believe in you.

Credit Mastery Habit #9:

Action Step: Pick one habit from the 800 Club to maintain and enhance your exceptional credit score.

In order to maintain and enhance your exceptional credit score, I'd suggest picking one habit from the 800 Club and sticking to it. You can start by setting up alerts for yourself, which will help you make sure that you're paying all of your bills on time (or even before they're due). You should also focus on keeping your credit utilization low, and building up a long credit history. Pay off your balances in full every month, and really show lenders that you're responsible with your credit. Try to be mindful of how many hard credit inquiries you make, and make it a regular habit to monitor your credit report for potential errors. In time, you should see your credit score start to climb!

SEGUE

Building up your credit score will take exceptional discipline and effort, but anyone can do it, no matter what their circumstance may be. Be patient and vigilant, and your hard work will eventually pay off. You might run into the occasional setback, but you shouldn't let that stop you from clawing your way out of the trenches and getting back on the right track. Now, I'd like to extend my congratulations because you've almost finished this book! In the next section, we'll wrap things up and tie everything together. By now, you should feel ready to take control of your financial health and send that credit score soaring!

CONCLUSION

I learned quite a lot while writing this book, and I hope you've learned a thing or two while reading it, too. I believe that building up your credit score — and nurturing it after the fact — is an art form. Unlike gourmet cooking or Picasso-esque painting, though, it's an art form that anyone can learn. Too many people won't even *try* to improve their financial health and get their credit scores up. The main reason for this is that they feel like it's impossible or that only rich people have good credit scores. There's also quite a bit of confusion surrounding credit scores, so it makes sense that most people would feel overwhelmed by the idea of increasing their credit scores.

Now that you've learned all about the components of your credit score and what the different sections on your credit report mean, you should be able to make more informed decisions when applying for credit cards or loans. You're well aware, by now, of the importance of checking your credit score regularly and how credit cards can affect your credit score. You also know the differences between good credit and bad credit and the red flags to keep an eye out for should you decide to hire a credit repair service.

We've gone over certain methods for building credit as someone who maybe doesn't have much of a credit history yet — such as using a secured credit card or piggybacking on someone else's good credit. You've also learned about the importance of monitoring your credit score when it comes to protecting yourself from identity theft, as well as some of the myths and misconceptions that prevent people from successfully building up their credit score.

You should be more than ready to embark on the journey of improving your credit score and building a healthy financial foundation for your future. Remember to adopt some of the habits that people in the 800 Club live by, and adjust your mindset if necessary to keep yourself motivated and vigilant throughout this process. You're one step closer to joining the Elite 800 Club, and I can't tell you how excited I am for you!

When my good friend, John, was struggling with his credit score, he sought advice from his dad — who had always been excellent with money. "I want to be debt-free and not have any credit cards," John told him in frustration. "But I can't even take out a car loan right now because I have such bad credit." His dad quickly realized that John had been managing his credit all wrong. He told him that he needed to rebuild his credit by applying for a credit card and paying off his balance in full every month, no matter what.

"It won't be easy," John remembers his dad saying. "But if you want to take out a car loan and eventually be free of debt, well — you don't have much of a choice. It'll be okay." John slowly but surely started to rebuild his credit. Over time, he found himself in the 600s and then, eventually, the 700s. Today, he's almost at the point where he can qualify for a new home, which he's extremely happy about. His story is yet another testament to the fact that you can do anything if you set your mind to it, no matter what life has thrown at you.

Now that you know all of the "super secret" insider tips and tricks when it comes to building up your credit score, it's time for you to focus on shifting your habits. As I've mentioned a few times now, this process is going to take a lot of time and effort, but you'll get there! If you've found the information in this book helpful, I'd greatly appreciate it if you left a review. Reviews from readers like you are ultimately what will help spread this information. Perhaps you have friends or family members who have poor credit as well, in which case you should let them know about this book so that they can get back on the right track. I wish you the best with your credit-building journey! Don't forget what you're fighting for, and keep on keepin' on.

YOU DID IT!

Congratulations on turning the final page of "Credit Score Mastery"! I'm thrilled that you chose to join me on this enlightening journey. I truly hope that the knowledge you've gathered has transformed your understanding of your financial capabilities.

Before we part ways, could I ask you for a small favor? Would you mind sparing a few moments to leave a review? Here's why your feedback is much more than just words:

Light the Way: Just like you were, there are many people standing at the start of their credit score journey, unsure of which direction to take. Your insights and experiences could be the guiding light they need to dive in!

Help Me Grow: I'm always looking to improve and evolve, and your thoughts are the invaluable wisdom I need. Did a particular chapter resonate with you? I'd love to hear about it.

Boost Our Community: You're now a valued member of a community of financially enlightened folks. Your journey, experiences, and reviews will inspire and empower others who are on the same path.

Here's how you can leave your review:

Star Power: On a scale of 1 to 5, how many stars would you give to your "Credit Score Mastery" adventure?

Spread the Word: Would you recommend this book to a friend or family member?

I can't thank you enough for choosing "Credit Score Mastery" as your guide. Your words and thoughts mean the world to me. I look forward to hearing about your experience.

Here's to your continued journey toward financial enlightenment!

RESOURCES

11 credit myths: Don't fall for 'em. Experian. (2021, August 24). https://www.experian.com/blogs/ask-experian/11-credit-myths-dont-fall-for-em/

The 3 main types of credit explained - self. credit builder. Self. (n.d.). https://www.self.inc/blog/types-of-credit

5 benefits of a secured credit card. M&T Bank - Personal & Business Banking, Mortgages, & More. (2023, April 20). https://www3.mtb.com/library/article/5-benefits-of-a-secured-credit-card

The 5 factors that make up your credit score. My Home by Freddie Mac. (n.d.). https://myhome.freddiemac.com/blog/notable/20210831-factors-credit-score

5 habits to get 800+ credit score. Consumer Credit. (2022, September 27). https://www.consumercredit.com/about-us/news-press-releases/2014/5-habits-to-get-800plus-credit-score/

Arford, K. (n.d.). *How to read a credit report*. Bankrate. https://www.bankrate.com/personal-finance/credit/how-to-read-a-credit-report/

Arghandewal, A. (2023, February 1). *How credit card piggybacking works*. Forbes. https://www.forbes.com/advisor/credit-cards/how-credit-card-piggybacking-works/

Better Money Habits. (2022, October 7). *What is a credit limit and why does it matter?*. Better Money Habits. https://bettermoneyhabits.bankofamerica.com/en/credit/understanding-your-credit-limit

Burchnell, T. (2023, March 3). *Common reasons people have bad credit*. EasyKnock. https://www.easyknock.com/blog/common-reasons-people-have-bad-credit

Camargo, M. (2023, January 26). *How to dispute an error on Your credit report*. Intuit Credit Karma. https://www.creditkarma.com/credit-cards/i/dispute-error-credit-report

Capital One. (2023, February 21). *How to use a credit card to build credit*.

Capital One. https://www.capitalone.com/learn-grow/money-management/how-to-use-a-credit-card-to-build-credit/

DeMatteo, M. (2023, May 9). *What's the difference between the "snowball" and the "avalanche" debt repayment methods?* CNBC. https://www.cnbc.com/select/debt-snowball-vs-debt-avalanche/

Dieker, N. (n.d.). *How credit inquiries affect your credit score.* Bankrate. https://www.bankrate.com/personal-finance/credit/how-credit-inquiries-affect-credit-score/

DiGangi, C. (n.d.). How credit impacts your life--your whole life | credit.com. https://www.credit.com/credit-reports/how-credit-impacts-your-day-to-day-life/

Irby, L. (2021, June 20). *How too much debt could be affecting your credit score.* The Balance. https://www.thebalancemoney.com/how-your-debt-affects-your-credit-score-960489

Johnson, H. D. (n.d.). *What is my credit score if I have no credit history?.* Bankrate. https://www.bankrate.com/personal-finance/credit/no-credit-score-zero-credit/

Luthi, B. (2022, July 11). *What credit monitoring can do for you.* Experian. https://www.experian.com/blogs/ask-experian/what-can-credit-monitoring-do-for-me/

Murphy, C. B. (2023, January 11). *Debt-to-income (DTI) ratio: What's good and how to calculate it.* Investopedia. https://www.investopedia.com/terms/d/dti.asp

Okerlund, A. (n.d.). *3 credit repair success stories and tips that will inspire you.* Best Company. https://bestcompany.com/credit-repair/blog/3-credit-repair-success-stories-and-tips-that-will-inspire-you

O'Brien, S. (2018, August 8). *Not checking your credit report comes with risks.* CNBC. https://www.cnbc.com/2018/08/07/not-checking-your-credit-report-comes-with-risks.html

O'Shea, B. (n.d.). *Identity theft: What it is, how to prevent it, warning signs and tips.* NerdWallet. https://www.nerdwallet.com/article/finance/how-to-prevent-identity-theft

Papandrea, D. (2022, March 30). *What is the credit utilization rule of thumb?.* The Balance. https://www.thebalancemoney.com/what-is-the-credit-utilization-rule-of-thumb-5115084

Papandrea, D. (n.d.). *65% think a credit card balance helps their score.* LendingTree. https://www.lendingtree.com/credit-cards/study/credit-card-mistakes-survey/

Peoplesfed. (2022, October 28). *Adopt a mindset that will help your money grow.* The People's Federal Credit Union. https://tpfcu.com/blog/adopt-mindset-will-help-money-grow/

Pierson, L. (2021, May 12). *Success story: Building credit from the bottom up.* Citizens Bank. https://www.citizens-banking.com/News-and-Resources/Article/success-story-building-credit-from-the-bottom-up-1

Pros and cons of having multiple credit cards in 2023. Compare & Apply for Credit Cards & Loan Online in India. (n.d.). https://www.bankbazaar.com/credit-card/pros-and-cons-of-multiple-credit-cards.html

Team, T. I. (2023, April 25). *Credit score: Definition, factors, and improving it.* Investopedia. https://www.investopedia.com/terms/c/credit_score.asp

What are the different types of credit scores?. LendingTree. (n.d.). https://www.lendingtree.com/credit-repair/what-are-the-different-types-of-credit-scores/

What is the difference between a credit score and a credit report. Equifax. (n.d.). https://www.equifax.com/personal/education/credit/report/difference-between-credit-score-vs-credit-report/

Made in the USA
Columbia, SC
06 September 2024

41924904R00096